Summersdale Publishers Ltd
46 West Street
Chichester
West Sussex
PO19 1RP
UK
www.summersdale.com

Printed and bound in the Czech Republic

ISBN: 978-1-84953-749-0

Substantial discounts on bulk quantities of Summersdale books are available to corporations, professional associations and other organisations. For details contact Nicky Douglas by telephone: +44 (0) 1243 756902, fax: +44 (0) 1243 786300 or email: nicky@summersdale.com.

# WINE

## THE ESSENTIAL GUIDE TO TASTING, HISTORY, CULTURE AND MORE

### CARO FEELY

summersdale

*Dedicated to my daughters Sophia and Ellie*

# CONTENTS

# NOTE FROM
# THE AUTHOR

• • • • • • • • • • • • • • • • • • • • • • • • • • • • • • • • • • • • • • • • • •

Thank you to Summersdale for asking me to write this book. As a wine lover, wine teacher, winemaker and writer, I jumped at the opportunity. Writing this book drew on my training as an educator for the Wine Spirit Education Trust and my work as a winegrower, and sent me to new places and many wonderful websites, where I discovered intriguing new facts about my beloved friend, wine. Two of the most useful websites were www.jancisrobinson.com (you can subscribe to a paid service but there is useful free information too) and www.winefolly.com. I highly recommend visiting both in your wine explorations.

# INTRODUCTION

'WINE CAN MAKE THE SAGE FROLIC
AND THE SERIOUS SMILE.'

HOMER'S *ODYSSEY*

••••••••••••••••••••••••••••••••••••••••••••••••••••••

Wine fills our mouths with flavour and our hearts with joy. The bounty of the vine has been called divine. Wine is an endless world and a wild companion, guaranteed to offer enlightenment, laughs and surprises. It can lift our spirits when we are down and provide the perfect way to celebrate when we are up. Today wine is embraced as part of the culture of enjoying food and even art – perhaps more now than ever throughout its long history.

But most of all it is something we share; whether it's a family lunch, a picnic, a book club event, a girls' night out or a lads' night in, the odds are that there is wine involved. Wine is a subject that we can never reach the end of; it is like an infinity joke: just when you think you've got it, you realise there is so much more.

My first taste of wine was a South African Riesling tingling with lime and exuding floral aromas. It offered a rainbow of flavours. From there I expanded into student fare, the cheapest red I could find and the odd special-occasion wine, then a friend who was a master of wine introduced me to a wider world that included international wines. I was smitten. Then I met my husband Sean, whose grandparents were winegrowers in South Africa. Our passion grew to such a point that wine became our profession. Now, as a winegrower, my wine view has expanded to include vines, the wonderful plants that give us grapes to make wine; the ground they grow in; the world of nature, balance and ecology that creates the best of wines and epitomises that French word *terroir*. Not to be confused with the 'terror' that one can feel when faced with a wall of wine, no explanations and an urgent requirement for a dinner-party bottle or two.

In this little book you will find an overview of the history of wine, advice on how to taste wine, details on wine regions, how wine is grown, *terroir*, a useful table of French wine terms and their English meanings (see pages 139–141) and more. Through it I hope that you will discover something new and perhaps a thirst to explore, to grab the joy of wine and not be afraid of using the wrong term, to try that unexplored wine area, grape or winemaker. After all, as a Latin saying goes:

'IT IS WELL TO REMEMBER THAT THERE ARE FIVE REASONS FOR DRINKING WINE: THE ARRIVAL OF A FRIEND; ONE'S PRESENT OR FUTURE THIRST; THE EXCELLENCE OF THE BEVERAGE; OR ANY OTHER REASON.'

# CHAPTER 1

# THE HISTORY OF WINE

'QUICKLY, BRING ME A BEAKER OF WINE, SO THAT I MAY WET MY MIND AND SAY SOMETHING CLEVER.'

ARISTOPHANES (COMIC PLAYWRIGHT OF ATHENS)

• • • • • • • • • • • • • • • • • • • • • • • • • • • • • • • • • • • • • • • • • • • • • • •

Since ancient times wine has been part of our culture. No other beverage has created such excitement and emotion throughout its vast history. Not only does it have a long, established history – the earliest archaelogical proof of wine made from grapes has been found in Georgia, Iran and China, currently dated to around 7000 BC – but also an interesting dimension that includes art and literature. Wine transcends the more basic food products and even fermented products like beer. It has a spiritual quality that caused it to be featured in the art of palaces and pyramids.

From the continent of Asia, wine moved slowly westwards across the map of antiquity into Europe and eventually to the New World. Now grapes are grown and wine is made across the globe, and the New World is creating its own wine history.

## A CATALYST FOR THE DISCOVERY OF WINE

The creation of pottery around 11,000 BC is thought to be a key technical innovation that enabled the creation of wine a few thousand years later.

## ARCHAEOLOGICAL DISCOVERIES AND THE OLD TESTAMENT

Archaeological proof shows winemaking going back over 9,000 years. It is mentioned in Genesis in the Bible, when Noah grows a vineyard, and thereafter features throughout the Old Testament.

## THE OLDEST WINERY

The oldest known winery was discovered in Armenia relatively recently, in 2007, and dates to around 4100 BC. The site includes an organised winemaking facility, complete with wine press, wine vats, jars and cups. Natural winemakers today use very similar tools, showing that winemaking is truly an ancient art. We could make wine successfully in that ancient winery.

## ANCIENT TIMES: GREECE AND EGYPT

Depictions of wine and winegrowing appeared in Ancient Greece from around 4500 BC and in Egypt from around 3500 BC. Etchings and paintings often included gods or religious symbols, indicating that wine held a spiritual status quite apart from other agricultural products.

## THE LEGEND OF THE DISCOVERY OF WINE

There are many legends surrounding wine. This legend about wine's origins is referenced in several places so is thought to have some credence. King Jamshid, an ancient king of Persia, banished a girl from his harem. She became depressed and tried to commit suicide, taking a jar that was marked 'poison' from one of the king's warehouses.

The jar contained rotting grapes but, luckily for her, the 'spoilage' was actually fermentation. After drinking the 'poison', the girl's spirit was lifted and she no longer felt like committing suicide. (What a wondrous liquid is wine!) Delighted, she took her discovery to the king, who was so taken with the new drink that he accepted the girl back into his harem and decreed that all grapes in his kingdom be devoted to winemaking henceforth. *Vive le vin!*

## ANCIENT TIMES: THE ROMAN EMPIRE

After Greece and Egypt, the next great wave was the Roman Empire, which spread vines and winemaking across Western Europe and into colder climates such as Germany and England. In France, vines were grown and wine was made well before the Romans arrived, but in the world-famous wine-producing region of Bordeaux, Ausonius, a famous Roman poet and aide to Caesar, did plant the first vines of St-Emilion in the fourth century AD.

## THOSE CLEVER ROMANS

Along with their houses with running water and underfloor heating, the Romans contributed significantly to wine's cause through research on grape varietals, weather, growing conditions and winemaking. This included advancing the design of the wine press and the storage of wine in barrels (originally invented by the Gauls) and glass bottles (originally invented by the Syrians) to complement their already widespread use of clay amphorae (jugs with a narrow neck and two handles). The Romans' wine activities were extensively documented in agricultural writings, such as *Rustica*, a set of 12 volumes on farming by Columella, who lived *c.* AD 4–70.

## WINE-LOVING MONKS

With the fall of the Roman Empire, the Dark Ages settled across Europe. It was the Roman Catholic Church, and particularly the monasteries, that kept the tradition of winegrowing and winemaking alive into the Middle Ages. Wine was needed for the religious ceremony of Mass but was also a valuable commodity. Many of the most famous French wine regions – including Burgundy, Champagne and parts of Bordeaux – were heavily influenced by monks. The Benedictine monks became some of the largest wine producers in France and Germany, followed by the Cistercians.

## CHAMPAGNE MOMENTS

The famous quote 'Come quickly... I'm tasting the stars!' is attributed to Dom Pérignon, a Benedictine monk, at the moment he discovered champagne.

## WINE AND SOCIAL STATUS

Wine was drunk by most of the population in the hotter climates where wine was produced, but in the cooler parts of Northern France, Belgium, Holland and the UK, beer was more widespread and wine was a luxury product. Like most fermented products – including sauerkraut, cheese and beer – wine was a way of storing harvest bounty for longer than the fresh product. It was delicious but also a handy way of providing calories and vitamins for the winter in a world without refrigeration and high-speed transport.

## WINE'S EXPANSION TO THE NEW WORLD

From the fifteenth century, wine production and consumption grew with the expansion into the Americas, South Africa, Australia and New Zealand. In the Americas, the Spanish extensively established vineyards and winemaking in the sixteenth century. In South Africa the first grapevines were planted by the founder of Cape Town, Jan van Riebeeck, in 1659.

In wine circles the New World is generally considered to be the USA, Australia, Argentina, Chile, South Africa and New Zealand; and the Old World is France, Spain, Italy, Germany, Portugal, Greece, Austria, Switzerland and Romania.

## VINEYARD DEVASTATION IN EUROPE

In the second half of the nineteenth century a phylloxera louse infestation destroyed many vineyards. The critter came from America and the devastation it caused was finally halted by grafting European vines (*Vitis vinifera*) on to American rootstock (*Vitis labrusca*). Today almost all vineyards in Europe are on American rootstock.

## THE NEW WORLD GAINS GROUND

While Western Europe, particularly France, was traditionally considered the leader in wine quality, the New World found its feet in the 1970s, when Californian wines garnered acclaim and won a high-profile blind tasting against the top wines of France. Since then, the New World's contribution to global production has increased to about half of the Old World's output – and it continues to grow.

# THE HISTORY OF WINE

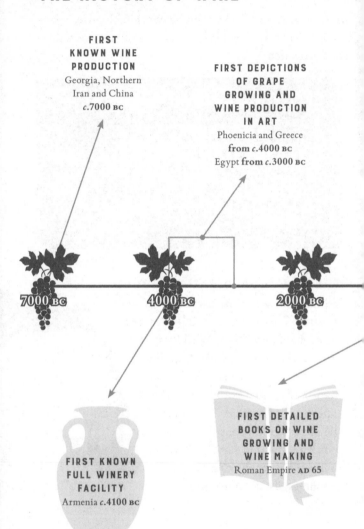

**FIRST KNOWN WINE PRODUCTION**
Georgia, Northern Iran and China
*c.*7000 BC

**FIRST DEPICTIONS OF GRAPE GROWING AND WINE PRODUCTION IN ART**
Phoenicia and Greece
**from** *c.*4000 BC
Egypt **from** *c.*3000 BC

7000 BC  4000 BC  2000 BC

**FIRST KNOWN FULL WINERY FACILITY**
Armenia *c.*4100 BC

**FIRST DETAILED BOOKS ON WINE GROWING AND WINE MAKING**
Roman Empire AD 65

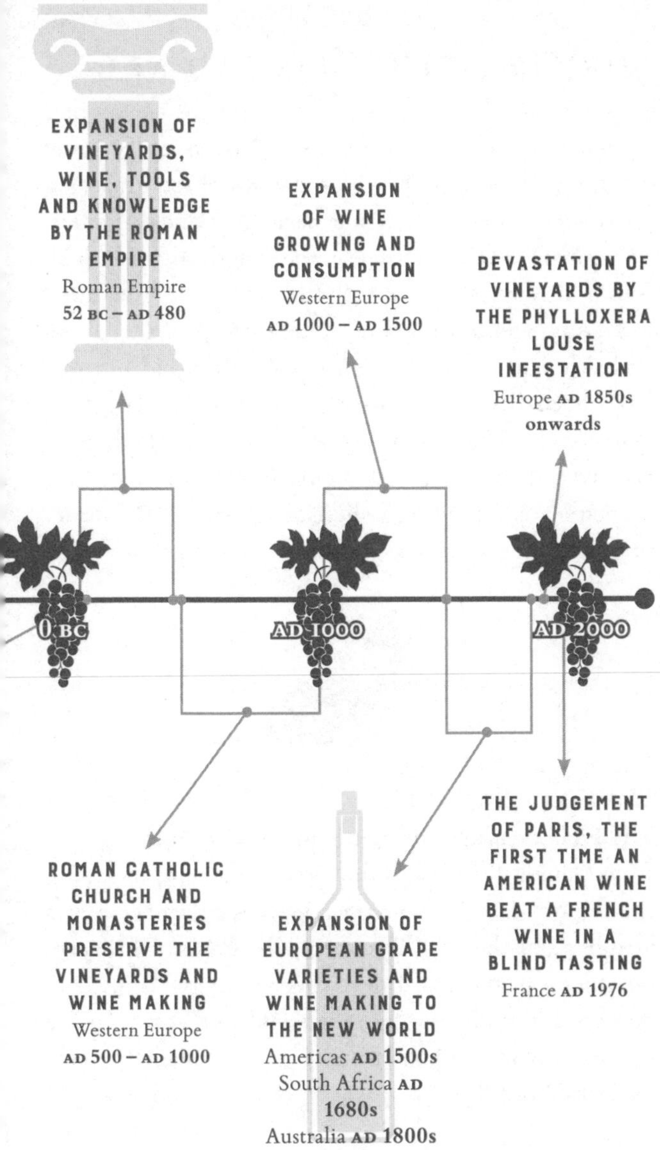

EXPANSION OF
VINEYARDS,
WINE, TOOLS
AND KNOWLEDGE
BY THE ROMAN
EMPIRE
Roman Empire
52 BC – AD 480

EXPANSION
OF WINE
GROWING AND
CONSUMPTION
Western Europe
AD 1000 – AD 1500

DEVASTATION OF
VINEYARDS BY
THE PHYLLOXERA
LOUSE
INFESTATION
Europe AD 1850s
onwards

0 BC

AD 1000

AD 2000

ROMAN CATHOLIC
CHURCH AND
MONASTERIES
PRESERVE THE
VINEYARDS AND
WINE MAKING
Western Europe
AD 500 – AD 1000

EXPANSION OF
EUROPEAN GRAPE
VARIETIES AND
WINE MAKING TO
THE NEW WORLD
Americas AD 1500s
South Africa AD
1680s
Australia AD 1800s

THE JUDGEMENT
OF PARIS, THE
FIRST TIME AN
AMERICAN WINE
BEAT A FRENCH
WINE IN A
BLIND TASTING
France AD 1976

# WINE IN LITERATURE AND ART

Looking at the original images of half-man, half-goat creatures dancing as they picked and pressed grapes on an Ancient Greek jar dating back thousands of years, you can feel awe-inspired at the length and depth of wine's history. Wine has been the subject of, or featured in, many works of poetry, literature and art. From prehistory to modern times, wine's effect and intrigue have been discussed. During the Renaissance, wine was widely depicted in art and literature. Perhaps it was even thanks to a little liquid inspiration that there is such a wide-ranging collection of art and literature surrounding this hallowed drink.

## WINE IN THE BIBLE

The Bible mentions vineyards and wine in many places, from Genesis through to the New Testament, including the famous tale of Jesus turning water into wine at a wedding. In the Old Testament, the book of Proverbs provides a plethora of fine sayings, such as: 'Wine is as good as life to man, if it be taken moderately; what is life to a man that is without wine? For it was made to make men glad.' Indeed.

## WINE IN ANCIENT GREEK LITERATURE

Many famous wine quotations are attributed to the epic poet Homer, who lived in the ninth century BC. He used wine in numerous descriptions, for example 'the wine-dark sea' was a phrase often used to describe a calm sea at dusk. That has become the subject of great debate among academics. What did he mean? Was their wine blue? Or was the sea red with algae? For me, there is little to debate – if you have seen a dark red sunset reflected on a calm sea, you will know what he meant.

## WINE IN LITERATURE IN THE ROMAN EMPIRE

During the reign of the Roman Empire, Ausonius, a Gallo-Roman, wrote much poetry about wine, in addition to creating Ausone, a prestigious estate that survives to this day in St-Emilion in France. In one poem, written in the fourth century AD, he even admits to being tipsy: 'It is outrageous that a strictly abstemious reader should sit in judgement on a poet a little drunk.'

## WINE IN ANCIENT CHINESE LITERATURE

A Chinese poet of the eighth century AD, who is commonly referred to as Li Bai or Li Po, wrote some of the most magical wine poems I have come across. 'Drinking Alone Beneath the Moon' is a divine piece where the language, in its original state, shimmers like an Impressionist painting. Alone, he pours a glass, then makes a threesome with the moon and his own shadow. They sing and dance, then scatter to reunite sometime in the future with the stars on the far side of the Milky Way. It is glorious.

## WINE ACCORDING TO THE MIGHTY SHAKESPEARE

William Shakespeare, one of the greatest writers of all time, devoted many words to wine and used wine to illustrate ideas. He echoed the age-old saying *in vino veritas* in silken words: 'The wine-cup is the little silver well, Where truth, if truth there be, doth dwell.' But one of his most cited quotes about alcohol comes from *Macbeth* Act II Scene III: '[Drink]: it provokes the desire, but it takes away the performance.'

## WINE IN GOLDEN-AGE LITERATURE

Literature in the golden age of wine reflected its importance. 'Wine is bottled poetry,' wrote Robert Louis Stevenson in the nineteenth century. In the same era, Leo Tolstoy used wine as a metaphor in *Anna Karenina*. Anna was 'drunk with the wine of the rapture she inspired' in the Count, her future lover.

## WINE IN MODERN LITERATURE

In the twentieth century American writer and Francophile Ernest Hemingway sang wine's praises in *Death in the Afternoon*, claiming that wine offered more enjoyment than any other sensory product that could be purchased. Then in his memoir, *A Moveable Feast*, he reflects that during his time in Europe drinking wine was as normal and necessary as eating.

A friend of Hemingway's, the great Irish writer James Joyce spoke of wine in his masterpiece *Ulysses*. His main character, Leopold Bloom, has a taste of wine that evokes a passionate memory. He refers to the wine generating a reflection on the sun's heat that also created the wine, which in turn evokes the memory of heated passion from his past. I recommend reading the book if only for this wondrous section.

More recently, Pablo Neruda's 'Ode to Wine' is a beautiful work that incites joy, passion and gratitude to the earth, nature and mankind, who together create wine. Ah yes! Wine evokes passion, art and dreams.

## WINE AND ART

Beautiful depictions of winemaking are found on walls of the pyramids in Egypt, dating to around 1500 BC. In Ancient Greece, art on frescoes and pottery give us an idea of wine's place in everyday life. Perhaps the most striking wine-related scenes are to be found on the black-figure-style pottery, and Exekias is thought to have been the master of this technique in the sixth century BC.

His Dionysus cup shows the god reclining in a boat surrounded by dolphins and with grapevines sprouting from the boat to fill the sky with bunches of grapes. From the same era, the Amasis painter's 'vintaging amphora' is a key piece that shows all the steps in winemaking carried out by large satyrs.

In Roman times, wine-related art decorated the walls in the villas of Pompeii and sculptured vines entwined the columns of the luxurious Gallo-Roman villa in Périgueux in the Dordogne in France, dating to around the first century AD.

Later, in medieval Europe, monastic art often depicted vines and wine. They show up in the decoration of manuscripts, stained glass and sculpture. The side door and part of the cloister of the fifteenth-century Eglise Collégiale of St-Emilion in France are decorated with bands of sculptured vine leaves.

## WINE LABEL ART

A wine business that has made a special feature of art is Château Mouton Rothschild in Pauillac, in the Bordeaux region of France. They have an impressive Wine in Art Museum that reaches back to Ancient Greece and Rome and goes forward to the modern day, including an extensive display of original artworks for their labels. Since 1945, the château each year has commissioned a famous artist to paint an image for the label of its grand vin (the first wine or highest quality wine, usually made from the best vineyards and vines that are at least 15 years old). Artists have included Marc Chagall, Salvador Dalí, Pablo Picasso, Francis Bacon, Jeff Koons – and even Prince Charles.

# WINE IN RELIGION

## THE ANCIENT WORLD

The changed state of consciousness created by wine was seen in a spiritual or religious light in the earliest Greek and Egyptian depictions of wine. The Ancient Greeks worshipped the god of wine Dionysus and the Romans followed that tradition with Bacchus.

### Bacchus/Dionysus, the great God of Wine

Bacchus is the Roman name for Dionysus, the Greek god of wine, fertility, grape harvest and intoxication of any form. Dionysus was the fruit of a union between the king of the gods, Zeus, and a mortal woman, Semele. He is thought to have been worshipped as far back as 1500 BC in Mycenaean Greece and Minoan Crete.

In the earliest portrayals Dionysus was bearded and mature, but most depictions show a young and handsome male figure, often nude, with a slightly feminine air. He is sometimes depicted with his followers, his 'thiasos', an ecstatic group of revellers including dancing humans, wild women and bearded satyrs with phalluses (erect penises) very much in evidence.

Bacchus is known as the liberator, the god whose wine, music and dance free his followers from fears, worries and self-conscious doubts. He also restrains the excesses of the super-powerful. We could all do with a bit of Bacchus in our worlds. He is the most referenced god in the world of wine, often depicted in wineries and barrel rooms.

## JUDAISM

Ritual wine for ceremony is part of Jewish practice and, as already explained, wine exists in Bible stories from the earliest of times. When Noah returns to dry earth after the Flood, for example, he becomes a farmer and plants a vineyard (Genesis 9:20). He later gets drunk and, while asleep, inadvertently exposes himself to his son Ham, leading to a harsh curse on Ham's son, Canaan.

## CATHOLICISM

With the dawning of Christianity, wine was invested with new and powerful symbolism in the Eucharist service, the celebration of Jesus' Last Supper and everlasting life. In this ceremony, bread (representing the body of Christ) and wine (representing his blood) are consecrated and consumed, so keeping wine flowing after the fall of the Roman Empire was necessary for this service to continue, and the Church and monasteries were willing and able to provide it.

## PROTESTANTISM

The Catholic monks in Europe were fully behind the creation and enjoyment of wine, but the Protestant movement tried to stem the tide, eventually going as far as generating Prohibition, the restriction of the sale of alcohol from 1920 to 1933 in the USA – an event to which the seventeenth-century French clergyman Cardinal Richelieu would have had a splendid riposte had he still been alive: 'If God forbade drinking, would He have made wine so good?'

### A PIONEER OF WINE DISTILLATION

Jabir ibn Hayyam (known as Geber in the Western World) was one of the great Islamic intellectuals of the eighth century AD, pioneering the distillation of wine for medicinal and industrial purposes and for perfume.

# THE ETYMOLOGY OF WINE WORDS

Reflecting all this weight of history, many wine terms can trace their origins back to ancient times.

## RAISE A TOAST

The tradition of raising a 'toast' originated in Rome, when the Senate ordered that Emperor Augustus (63 BC– AD 14) be honoured at every meal. At that time, a piece of burnt toast, or *tostus*, was often dropped into a glass of wine just before drinking it in order to create a smoked aroma. It was almost like an ancient form of the oaking that is done today with toasted barrels. Just after dropping the toast into the wine, guests would raise their glasses to Augustus. This later extended to 'toasting' the guest of honour, and eventually became the custom found at most weddings and official celebrations today.

### TOASTING AND AVOIDING LETHAL POISON

In Ancient Greece, each guest was 'toasted' with a ceremonial drink of wine at the start of the evening. Rather than toast with individual cups, however, everyone drank from a communal bowl to ensure the wine wasn't poisoned. At the time, poison was a common way to get rid of enemies or to avoid paying debts.

## RULE OF THUMB

Before the invention of thermometers, brewers would dip a thumb or finger into the liquid to determine the optimum temperature for adding yeast, hence the term 'rule of thumb'.

## SYMPOSIUM

'Symposium' has nothing to do with academics meeting to discuss calculus, medicine or Ancient Hebrew. It originated in Ancient Greece and means 'drinking together'. Symposia were typically held in men's quarters and participants were served wine, food and dancing girls, as they reclined on couches while 'debating' politics and philosophy. A symposium was coordinated by a 'symposiarch', a kind of sommelier, who decided the strength of the wine after considering the seriousness of the debate. Wine was almost always mixed with water; pure wine was considered to be appropriate only for the 'uncivilised'.

## CONCLUSION

Wine's rich heritage, and its historical association with art and literature, spans millennia. This liquid sustenance transports us, inspires us and provokes dreams. What makes it so? Why is it so complex and resplendent? It is because wine is a natural product; it is a connection to the earth and the sky. If we take the time to listen, we can hear the whispers of the stars. And if we take the time to consider it, we can understand why wine has featured in so many works of art and literature.

# CHAPTER 2

# WINE TASTING

'WHO KNOWS HOW TO TASTE
NEVER DRINKS WINE AGAIN
BUT TASTES SECRETS.'

SALVADOR DALÍ

••••••••••••••••••••••••••••••••••••••••••••••••••

Wine tasting offers great enjoyment. In our tasting room and wine school I often hear: 'Until today I thought wine tasting was a load of nonsense, reserved for wine snobs!'

Sometimes I am asked if we winemakers add cinnamon or orange zest or mint to our wine. No. Then why do wines display so many different aromas? Why is wine made with grapes and not with oranges or apples?

Grapes have thousands of polyphenols (the aroma compounds that tell us a fruit's character and flavour), whereas apples and oranges only have a couple of hundred. It is this breadth of flavour, this rainbow of characteristics – that vary based on climate, soil, grape type, and how we farm and make the wine – that makes wine tasting so interesting. (In Europe the word 'wine' is reserved for grape wine. Other fruit wines are alcoholic drinks rather than wine.)

Taking time to appreciate a wine – to sniff and swirl – is a form of respect: respect for the work that went into the product; for the nature and sunlight that created it; and for yourself. When we enjoy a glass or two of wine in this way we are unlikely to become drunk or binge-drink.

So how do we wine-taste?

## THE ART OF WINE TASTING

When we wine-taste we are like detectives. We are investigating the wine, trying to hear its secrets, discovering what it can tell us about itself. We divine clues about wine from three sensory areas: look, smell and taste. As we gather the clues, we cross-check and make our final assessment based on corroborating evidence across the three senses. It can be great fun. Blind tasting is the school of humility as even the greatest tasters in the world are regularly surprised.

We taste wine for the enjoyment of it, as a way of remembering the wine, to understand what we like or don't like about a wine so as to choose better in the future, or to be able to describe the wine to a friend, on a blog, to a local wine shop owner or our significant other.

## THE TASTING PLACE AND THE TASTER

Ideally you should be in a neutral environment with no strong smells, with a white background and good light for looking at the wine.

You should come to the tasting with a clear palate, so if, for example, you recently had a coffee, drink a glass of water and swoosh it around to cleanse your mouth, otherwise the wine will taste of coffee.

Neutral air is important during a tasting, so avoid strongly scented toiletries and make-up. A blast of powerful perfume or aftershave will destroy a fine bouquet, and kitchen smells (such as garlic, onion or spices cooking) will mask fine aromas.

## THE GLASSWARE

Good crystal glasses are essential. A glass with a tulip shape that is wider at the bottom and tighter at the top to funnel the aromas, on a stem and made of fine quality glass is best. It sounds very wine geeky but it is like listening to music on a tiny speaker compared to a proper sound system if you use the wrong glass; the song that is playing is the same, but the experience is completely different. Top glass producers like Riedel (who also produce a lower-priced alternative called Spiegelau) have perfected the art of making your wine sing.

## THE EYE: THE LOOK OF THE WINE

Pour a tasting sample into your glass. A sample is usually about a third of the glass, which means that most tasting glasses are filled to about the widest point – enough to experience the wine and to give a good swirl – but don't swirl just yet.

First, take the glass and look at the colour against the white background. This will help you to discover something about the style, health and age of the wine. Hold the glass sideways, think about the colour at the core (the middle) versus the rim. If it is a white wine, is it water white (almost clear), lemon, gold or even amber? If it is a red wine, is it purple, ruby, garnet or brick red? Is it light or deep in colour?

## A FEW POINTERS ABOUT THE LOOK OF THE WINE:

- Wine browns with age, especially at the rim, so this can offer a clue to the vintage (the year the grapes were picked).

- If the wine is cloudy or fizzing when you don't expect it to be it could be an indication of something gone wrong, that the health of the wine has been compromised by something, e.g. a bad closure.

- The depth of colour can help narrow down the variety and/or the region. For example, a Pinot Noir from Burgundy is usually lighter in colour than a Merlot/Cabernet Sauvignon blend from Bordeaux, while a young Cabernet Sauvignon is more purple than a young Merlot.

## THE LEGS, OR TEARS, OF THE WINE

I often hear 'Look at those legs!' and we're not talking about the pretty girl in the miniskirt. The 'legs' or 'tears', the way the wine runs back down the glass after swirling it around, have nothing to do with quality. They have more to do with alcohol content and/or residual sugar. You can find very light, very high-quality white wine with very little by way of 'legs', and very high-alcohol, bad-quality wine with marked legs.

## THE NOSE OF THE WINE

Now take a good deep sniff – don't hold back – and let the aromas go right up into the back of your nose and into your brain. Then do a good swirl and do that again. You should find a little evolution between the first nose (before you swirled) and the second nose (after you swirled). Sometimes it is easier to identify a single aroma on the first nose and the second nose becomes complex, perhaps even a little crowded and confusing with some alcohol aromas. Note what you pick up on both. Even wine words sound good: the legs, the swirl!

### THE THREE NOSES

In France we talk of three noses: the first nose before you swirl, the second after swirling and the third on the empty glass. Often when the glass is empty we can pick up some evolution of the coating of wine that remains on the glass and it is easier to pick up minor faults – if there are any.

Does the wine smell clean? Or unpleasant/unclean? If so, this could be 'reduction' (lack of oxygen) and therefore not something serious, or it could be more serious and permanent like cork taint (see below). Is it weak or pronounced? Is it youthful or mature? Is it fruity, spicy, vegetal (vegetable or leaf aromas) or earthy? Or a mix of these?

## WINE FAULTS

'A little horse pee or dank cardboard with your wine, sir?'

There are many potential faults in wine. Here are four of the worst culprits:

- Cork taint or 2,4,6-Trichloroanisole (TCA): this usually comes from a cork gone bad and leaves your wine smelling and tasting like a damp basement, wet dog or dank cardboard. As a quick fix if it is very mild, you can pour the wine into a bowl, cover it with clingfilm and the film will attract some of the TCA. There is no health risk from cork taint; it just ruins your pleasure.

- Microbial problems like 'Brett': microbe problems can create bad smells like rotting cabbage and animal sweat or, worse, animal urine. One of the most widespread in wine is Brettanomyces (Brett), which can create a smell of stable. If you are unsure, give the wine a lot of air by pouring it into a wide-based decanter, or even shaking it up or beating it, before you throw it out. Sometimes a bad smell can be just 'reduction', don't forget, and will disappear with a good aeration.

- Volatile acidity: a smell of nail varnish, indicating that the wine has started to make its way towards vinegar. In small doses it can add complexity but too much usually is not good.

- Oxidation: the wine has a sherry-like nose and looks dull. If it is a young wine this could have happened with a mistake in the winemaking or through a bad cork.

41

## A YOUTHFUL BEAUTY OR AN ANCIENT SAGE?

Youthful wines offer fresh, fruity noses, whereas older wines offer more cooked fruit and earthy notes. Getting back to the wine in your glass, it is time to corroborate your evidence on the colour and the nose. For example, if it is a white wine that is light-lemon youthful in colour then the nose should be youthful fruity. Alternatively, if it is a red that is garnet or brick red on the edges of the rim of the wine in your glass, then the notes will probably be more cooked or dried fruit, and perhaps earthy and even leathery, as we can expect from a more mature wine. Then there are all the potential colours and aromas in between the wine just born and one that is an ancient sage. Practice makes perfect in this game of wine tasting, so keep testing yourself.

## THE GRAPE, THE ORIGIN AND WINEMAKING

As well as an idea of the wine's age, the aromas provide an idea of the varietal or grape type. The expression of the varietal(s) in varying climates and vintages will be different, so the aromas can also help you decipher where the grapes were grown. You can start to form an idea of the winemaking too. For example, barrel-ageing can offer woody, toasty, vanilla or coconut aromas.

## THE AROMAS OR THE BOUQUET OF THE WINE

We usually talk about 'aromas' when a wine is young and 'bouquet' when it is older and a little more complex. Wine writers might use other words like 'note' to indicate aroma.

### FRUITY AROMAS
**White fruits**, e.g. apple, pear
**Stone fruits**, e.g. apricot, peach
**Red fruits**, e.g. strawberry, redcurrant
**Black fruits**, e.g. blackberry, dark plum

### FLORAL AROMAS
e.g. rose, violet, honeysuckle, orange blossom

### HERBAL OR VEGETAL AROMAS
e.g. thyme, fennel, grassy, cabbage

### SPICY AROMAS
**Sweet spices**, e.g. clove, cinnamon
**Strong spices**, e.g. white pepper, black pepper

### OAK AROMAS
e.g. vanilla, smoke, grilled coffee, cocoa/chocolate

### NUT AROMAS
e.g. almonds, hazelnuts

### MINERAL AROMAS
e.g. smoky flintstone, salty limestone

### DAIRY AROMAS
e.g. cream, butter

## IT SMELLS LIKE WHITE/ RED WINE TO ME...

Do you find that all this talk of aromas reminds you of a strong stable smell? At first it is difficult to get our nose and brain to engage. Our brain wants to see what we are smelling, hence it sees white wine and says white wine. Try closing your eyes and taking a good sniff when you are in the kitchen opening a banana, cutting an apple, using the cinnamon or ginger, walking past a rose or even picking up your leather bag. Try to train your brain to work on associating aromas without seeing them. Then take an aromatic wine like Gewürztraminer and see what you find.

## GIVE THE WINE SOME TIME

You should give your wine a little time to open up. As it takes air in, it will evolve and give you different aromas. Both red and white wine can benefit from some air. In general, young red wine needs the most time to open up. To make life easy for yourself rather than decanting, pour a glass of wine out of the bottle to allow air in to the widest point of the bottle and then leave the cork out so the wine can take a little air.

## WHICH DECANTER TO USE AND WHEN?

If you have time to appreciate your wine over the course of the evening, there is no need to decant as it will be fun to see the evolution over time. However, if you have six people for dinner and the bottle will be finished after one pour, then decanting a young wine (particularly red) for aeration to ensure that the single pour is at its best can be a good idea. An old wine is too fragile to be decanted in this way. If an old wine is decanted, it should be carefully poured into a narrow decanter to remove the sediment and served soon after. A wide-bottom decanter will give it too much air and will kill an old wine.

## SERVING WINE AT THE RIGHT TEMPERATURE

Serving wine in good glasses and at the right temperature also contributes to your appreciation of it and your perception of its quality. Follow this simple serving guide:

- **White wine**: serve chilled between 6 and 10 degrees Celcius, using the cooler end of the range for lighter-style whites and the higher end for richer, barrel-aged whites.

- **Red wine**: serve between 16 and 18 degrees Celcius. (The commonly held view is that red wine should be served 'at room temperature' but today's heated houses are, in reality, often too hot for the ideal temperature range.) The exceptions are very-light-style reds, like Beaujolais, that can be served at around 12 degrees Celcius – i.e. served almost as cool as a white.

In very practical terms, for white wine, the temperature of your fridge is good. For reds, the fridge then on to the table (to rise a little from fridge temperature) in summer or a cool place in the house in winter is good. An ice bucket or cooler sleeve is a great way to keep your whites, rosés or sparkling cold once on the table.

## THE MOUTH: THE TASTE OF THE WINE

Now take a good sip and swirl it around inside your mouth. If you want to look like a real wine geek, you can suck a little air through the wine to experience the aromas more fully. To do this, hold the wine in your mouth, lean your head forward a little and then suck air through your teeth and through the wine to draw the aromas back up through your nose. It is called 'retro-olfactory' when you do this: that is, the aromas come into your nose through the back entrance instead of the front. To be tried at home with close family rather than on a blind date or in a Michelin-starred restaurant... When you swirl the wine around your mouth you will often pick up flavours that you would miss if you just drank it.

### TO SPIT OR NOT TO SPIT, THAT IS THE QUESTION...

I am often asked 'do you have to spit when wine tasting?' If you are tasting many wines or driving then, yes, you should spit the wine into the spittoon provided rather than swallowing. Wine professionals spit to keep their brains intact for the work of wine tasting. If you are only tasting a couple of wines and not driving, there is probably no need to spit, but if you want to get into serious wine tasting and learn about wine then you need to develop the spit reflex.

## THE COMPONENTS OF WINE

A wine is made up of many components that you can sense in your mouth. As you experience the wine, consider how it tastes and feels in your mouth.

Try to assess the following components:

- **The level of residual sugar**: the sweetness on your tongue, if any.

- **The acidity**: sense the acidity in the sides of your cheeks – your mouth will water if there is high acidity, like it does with lemon juice.

- **The alcohol**: you can sense high alcohol content by a burning sensation at the back of the throat and alcohol generally by the weight in the mouth. High alcohol can also offer a hint of sweetness.

- **The tannin**: the astringence or drying sensation on your gums and tongue. Think of what a strong cup of tea does to your tongue and gums.

- **The flavours**: what we think are flavours are actually aromas, so consider the main aroma families: fruity, spicy, vegetal or animal.

## THE TEXTURE AND SHAPE OF THE WINE

Think about the texture of the wine: is it smooth and soft? Or jagged and grainy? Think about the way it felt when it first hit your mouth (the attack), then the taste, texture and sensation in the middle (mid palate) and finally the finish. In the mid palate was it full-bodied, filling you with a round flavour, or was it light and more linear?

## THE FINISH OF THE WINE

Did the flavour remain in your mouth for a while after swallowing? For how long? Over four seconds is a medium finish, over ten seconds is a long finish and over twenty seconds is an exceptional finish. This is a key indicator of quality. A fine wine offers magic in the mid palate and the finish. It is easy to fake a pleasant attack with modern industrial winemaking techniques, but true quality and the real excitement in the mid palate or finish can only come from quality grapes that are the result of good practices in the vineyard.

## THE GRAPE OR THE *TERROIR*? WHAT MAKES A WINE WHAT IT IS?

Like the nose, the taste (and to a certain extent the look) of wine can help to decipher the grape. For example, if you have a high-acid, high-tannin red wine that has a note of cassis and a deep purple colour, it is likely to be Cabernet Sauvignon as these are all characteristics of a youthful Cabernet. However, what creates the taste of a wine is not just the grape type, but also the *terroir*, a miraculous combination of climate, soil and grape plus farming and winemaking.

## THE BALANCE AND COMPLEXITY OF THE WINE

Going a step further in your tasting assessment, you should also consider the wine's equilibrium and complexity. Some wines are light and fun while others are deep and complex. Does the wine have balance between its key components or does one stand out above the rest, for example high alcohol that overpowers its tannin and acidity? In your overall assessment of a wine you can consider these aspects as well as how it compares to others in its category and price range.

## CLASSIFYING THE WINE TYPE AND STRUCTURED WINE TASTING

Wine is generally classified according to these three categories:

1.  Colour (easy to see): red, rosé or white.
2.  Sweetness (easy to taste): dry (this means no or very little residual sugar i.e. less than 4 grams of residual sugar per litre, or 4 g/l – the wine can still seem rich and fruity); off-dry (some small amount of residual sugar, usually 4–12 g/l); medium-sweet (12–45 g/l); or full-sweet (more than 45 g/l).
3.  Sparkling or still (easy to see and taste): there are many different guises of sparkling wine, including real champagne, *méthode traditionelle* and 'manufactured'.

These are the starting points for classifying a wine in blind tasting. From there, you can delve deeper into more structured wine tasting. If you want to fine-tune your skills, a wine course with your local wine shop or through an organisation like the Wine Spirit Education Trust with one of their approved programme providers (such as my own WSET APP) can help you.

# GETTING TO KNOW THE GRAPE VARIETIES

Usually as a first step in a wine tasting course you are introduced to wines from specific grape varieties. It is a good place to start and this offers a base for branching into more complicated blended wines and *appellations*.

## COMMON VARIETIES OF GRAPE

There are hundreds of grape varieties – 1,368 confirmed grape varieties, to be exact – but relatively few are widely available and/or known.

For example, did you ever hear of Airén? It is the most planted white varietal in the world and the third most planted varietal after Cabernet Sauvignon and Merlot. It is also decreasing the fastest so it will probably be well down the list in the next few decades. As the most widely planted grape in Spain, Airén has probably formed part of a Spanish wine you have tasted in the past without you realising it was there.

# THE TOP TEN WINE GRAPE VARIETALS WORLDWIDE

**1**   **Cabernet Sauvignon**
a red varietal (6.3 per cent of the market)

**Merlot**   **2**
a red varietal (5.81 per cent)

**3**   **Airén**
a white varietal (5.48 per cent)

**Tempranillo**   **4**
a red varietal (5.05 per cent)

**5**   **Chardonnay**
a white varietal (4.32 per cent)

**Syrah/Shiraz**   **6**
a red varietal (4.03 per cent)

**7**   **Grenache/Garnacha Tinta**
a red varietal (4.01 per cent)

**Sauvignon Blanc**   **8**
a white varietal (2.39 per cent)

**9**   **Trebbiano Toscano / Ugni Blanc**
a white varietal (2.39 per cent)

**Pinot Noir**   **10**
a red varietal (1.88 per cent)

Hectares planted as share of total global vineyards in 2010.

Source of figures: Anderson, K. and Aryal, N., Database of Regional, National and Global Winegrape Bearing Areas by Variety, 2010, Wine Economics Research Centre, University of Adelaide, December 2013, revised July 2014.

## THE TOP GRAPES AND THEIR
## TYPICAL CHARACTERISTICS

There are telltale characteristics that can help you detect whether your red tipple is a Cabernet Sauvignon or a Pinot Noir, and whether your white is a Chardonnay or a Sauvignon Blanc – or perhaps even a Négrette red or a Godello white.

When looking at the wine wall in your local shop, don't be put off if you don't recognise the varietal. Some of the most exciting wines being made today are from ancient and little-known heritage varietals; not only is this good for biodiversity but it keeps your wine interesting.

# THE TOP TEN WHITE VARIETALS (IN ORDER OF GLOBAL PLANTING) AND THEIR CHARACTERISTICS

1. **Airén**: A neutral white grape of Spain that is losing ground to red Tempranillo. Specific aromas can include citrus and apple.

2. **Chardonnay**: Originated in France and made famous by the quality whites of Burgundy. Usually full and soft, but specific *terroirs* like Chablis can be sharp and flinty. Aromas include apple, peach, pear, pineapple, citrus, melon and butter. Often barrel-aged, hence it can have oak aromas like vanilla.

3. **Sauvignon Blanc**: Originated in France with wines like Sancerre but now famous as the signature grape of New Zealand. Invigorating and acidic. Aromas include grass, gooseberry, passion fruit, lychee, asparagus and grapefruit.

4. **Trebbiano Toscano** (also known as **Ugni Blanc** in France): Originated in Italy. Highly productive, resistant to disease and pests, and high in acidity. It is widely used in brandy. Tangy with citrus and peach or melon aromas, it can also have floral notes.

5. **Grasevina**: Thought to have originated in Central Europe and most widely planted there. Also called 'Romantic Riesling' but it is not related to Riesling. Offers a mild wine with fruity and floral aromas.

6. **Rkatsiteli**: Originated in Georgia. One of the oldest grape varieties. It offers an acidic white wine with spicy and floral aromas.

7. **Riesling**: Originated in Germany and widely planted there. Lively and acidic. Specific aromas can include apple, lime, passion fruit and petrol.

8. **Macabeo** (also called **Viura** or **Macabeu**): Originated in Spain. Like Chardonnay it can display a variety of styles: fresh, aromatic and floral if harvested early, but full with honey and nut aromas if harvested later and aged in oak. It is a key grape in white Rioja.

9. **Cayetana Blanca**: Widely planted in Spain for brandy production. It offers neutral wines.

10. **Aligoté**: Found in Burgundy, France and Central Europe. High in acidity. Aromas include apple, lemon and herbal notes.

## OTHER WELL-KNOWN WHITE GRAPES

Other white grapes that are popular and well known, but not as widely planted, include:

- **Pinot Gris/Pinot Grigio:** Aromas such as lime, lemon, apple, pear and peach. Can include floral notes like honeysuckle. This grape is popular, and consumption and planting have grown rapidly in recent years.

- **Chenin Blanc:** Can produce high quality but also can be bland if farmed for volume. It offers greengage, angelica and honey notes.

- **Sémillon:** Smooth with specific aromas including peach, apple, citrus, honey and toast.

- **Gewürztraminer:** Usually rich and almost oily with exotic, spicy notes and specific aromas like ginger, cinnamon, lychees and rose.

- **Viognier:** The white grape of the Rhône valley that is rising in popularity in the New World. It offers a lush floral wine with specific aromas of violet, pear, apricot and peach.

# THE TOP TEN RED VARIETALS (IN ORDER OF GLOBAL PLANTING) AND THEIR CHARACTERISTICS

1. **Cabernet Sauvignon**: Originated in France. High acid, high tannin. It offers an intense wine with ageing potential and is often oaked. Specific aromas include blackcurrant (cassis), cedar, green pepper, mint, chocolate, tobacco and cigar box.

2. **Merlot**: Originated in France. A medium acid, medium tannin, full-bodied wine offering rich, plummy, spicy notes that blends well with Cabernet Sauvignon, the classic Bordeaux blend. Other specific aromas include fruitcake, Christmas pudding, blackberry and pencil shavings.

3. **Tempranillo**: Originated in Spain. Relatively full-bodied but low in acid and sugar, therefore often blended with other varietals like Grenache for sugar and Carignan for acid. Aromas include plum and berry, and with age include leather, herbs and tobacco.

4. **Syrah (or Shiraz)**: Originated in France. A rich, spicy style with high tannin and full body. Specific aromas include raspberry, blackberry, pepper, clove and spice, and with age include leather, game and tar.

5. **Grenache (Garnacha)**: Thought to have originated in Spain. A high sugar (high alcohol), low tannin and low acid grape. Specific aromas include strawberry and blackcurrant, then tobacco and dried apricot with age.

6. **Pinot Noir**: Originated in France. Fragrant and silky, red fruit and sometimes gamey complexity. Specific aromas include raspberry, strawberry, cherry, violet, rose, game, cabbage/manure (with age).

7. **Carignan (or Mazuelo)**: Thought to have originated in Spain. High in acid and tannin and can be bitter. Best as a blending partner but can offer interesting dark fruit, spice and liquorice.

8. **Bobal**: Originated in Spain. Deep colour with high acid and tannin. Dark fruit and spice aromas. Usually a blending partner. The name comes from the Latin *bovale* in reference to the grape bunches that are shaped like a bull's head.

9. **Sangiovese**: Originated in Italy. The name apparently comes from the Latin *sanguis Jovis*, the blood of the King of the Gods. It is high acid and medium to high tannin, with a bright colour in youth. Aromas include sour cherry, strawberry, tea leaf and, with age, earth and tar.

10. **Mourvèdre (or Monastrell or Mataró)**: Originated in France/Italy. High tannin and medium to high alcohol. The aromas are soft red fruit but can also be gamey and earthy. It is a difficult grape but in the right conditions can produce magnificent wine.

## OTHER WELL-KNOWN RED GRAPES

Next in line are these red grapes:

- **Cabernet Franc:** Medium-bodied and floral with specific aromas including green peppers, redcurrant, chocolate and flowers.

- **Malbec (Côt):** Deep colour and high tannin with specific aromas including plum and anise.

Not so widely planted but with a good international following are:

- **Nebbiolo:** Made famous by the Barolo wine of Italy with its dark cherry, rose, tar and chocolate notes.

- **Zinfandel:** Famous in California; the same grape as the Italian Primitivo. Full-bodied, rich, smoky and spicy.

- **Pinotage:** A South African grape that was a cross between Cinsault and Pinot Noir, offering dark plum and blackberry aromas with savoury, spicy and smoky notes.

# A WINE FOR EVERY MOOD, PERSONALITY AND EVENT

What sort of wine lover are you? An introverted 'iron fist in a velvet glove' like a Burgundy Pinot Noir, or an extroverted, passionate powerhouse throwing it all out there like a premium Napa Cabernet Sauvignon? There are wines for every mood, personality and event. Part of the fun of wine is that there is so much variety.

Even if you know you love New Zealand Sauvignon Blanc, don't stop there: try Sauvignon from Sancerre or Bergerac, try another crisp wine like vinho verde, then keep on expanding your explorations.

Why not make it your mission to try a totally new wine for every two old favourites?

## WHAT KIND OF TASTE BUDS DO YOU HAVE?

There is a world of variety in wine lovers, as with wine itself. We are all different: the number of tastebuds we have differs, and how we perceive tastes differs. Knowing your tastes means you can more easily select wines you will like.

# WHAT KIND OF TASTER ARE YOU? THREE TASTE PROFILES

| Taster Type | Strong (tolerant) | Medium (sensitive) | Light (very sensitive) |
|---|---|---|---|
| **Your general flavour preferences** | You like strongly flavoured foods and drinks. | You enjoy many different foods and drinks and some intense flavours but not bitterness. | You don't like strong flavours and bitterness. |
| **Your hot drink/cold dessert preferences** | You choose espresso or very strong tea and perhaps lime sorbet for dessert. | You prefer medium-strength coffee/tea with milk and would likely go for the vanilla ice cream over the lime sorbet (at least some of the time). | You prefer a latte or very delicate teas, perhaps with milk and sugar, and vanilla ice cream over lime sorbet. |

| Wines you prefer or might enjoy if you haven't tried them already | You will like strong wines high in tannin, oak and alcohol – example grapes include Cabernet Sauvignon and Pinotage. On the whites you will enjoy the dry, acidic styles, perhaps Sancerre or a vinho verde. | You will like rounder-style red wines, perhaps warm-climate Syrah/Shiraz, and perhaps full-bodied whites like Chardonnay. | You will like more delicate and perhaps floral kinds of white wines, off-dry or even semi-sweet like Riesling or Pinot Grigio, and in red wine you will like lower tannin styles like Pinot Noir and perhaps Grenache. |
|---|---|---|---|

## WINES FOR MOODS AND OCCASIONS

Wine is adaptable to your mood and to the occasion. Here are some recommended matches to try out.

| The mood | A matching style of wine |
| --- | --- |
| An upbeat mood or a celebration | Sparkling wine. Champagne or *méthode traditionelle*. |
| Sharp and witty | Dry white wine. Perhaps a Sauvignon Blanc. |
| Generous and loving | Rich white. Perhaps a barrel-aged Chardonnay. |
| Sad | Sweet or dessert wine. Jane Austen recommended Vin de Constance, a South African dessert wine, as a cure for a broken heart. |
| Introverted and sensitive | A light red. Perhaps a Beaujolais. |
| Contemplative and poetic | A medium red like Burgundy Pinot Noir. |
| Extroverted and outgoing | A heavy, big, bold red like Cabernet Sauvignon from California or Malbec from Argentina. |
| Pensive or a dinner with your boss | Classic Bordeaux – perhaps *grand cru classé*. |
| Relaxed and casual | Rosé |

········································································

## CONCLUSION

Wine tasting can be both fun and educational. Once you train your nose a little you will get so much more out of your glass of wine. Knowing the key grape varietals is often the first step for a wine lover but, since many wines are blends or grapes you may not know, sticking to only one or two grape varietals will limit your enjoyment. After all, the varietal is just one part of the complex web of a wine; just as important are the climate, the soil and then the winemaking.

········································································

## CHAPTER 3

# GRAPE GROWING AND ITS EFFECT ON THE WINE

'WINE IS SUNLIGHT, HELD TOGETHER BY WATER.'

GALILEO GALILEI

• • • • • • • • • • • • • • • • • • • • • • • • • • • • • • • • • • • • • • • •

Vines are miraculous things. They create 94 per cent of their dry matter from what they get from the sky, so what happens with the weather has a dramatic effect on them. A Chardonnay from Chablis in the north of France tastes quite different (lemon, apple and flint aromas) from a Chardonnay growing in the south of France (tropical fruit aromas).

Taken at its most basic level, the amount of sun and heat influences how much sugar and acid there are in the grape. More sun equals more sugar (hence usually more alcohol, since the sugar is converted to alcohol in the process of making wine) and less acid. Less sun means the opposite. Therefore we can expect lighter wines in colder places like Germany and heavier wines in hotter places along the Mediterranean like Languedoc.

# THE GRAPES AND WHERE TO FIND THEM

## WHAT ARE GRAPES?

A grape is made of skin, pulp and pips. In the pulp we find the liquid which holds the sugars, acids and some flavours. In the skin we find colour, tannin and aroma compounds. In the pips are bitter oils which we generally don't want in wine.

# ANATOMY OF A GRAPE

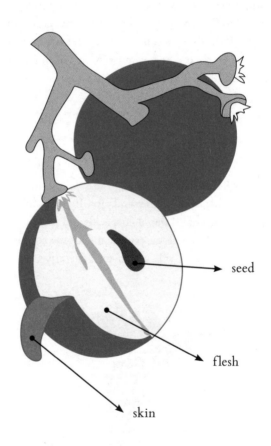

seed

flesh

skin

## TOUPEES, MOVE OVER. HERE COMES GRAPE SEED OIL.

When it is cold-pressed, grape seed oil can be a healthy and light-tasting alternative to other seasoning and cooking oils. It is thought to increase good cholesterol levels and decrease the bad. It is highly prized for cosmetics because of its light touch. It can be used as a shaving lubricant and even as a growth and strengthening treatment for hair.

## VINEYARDS OF THE WORLD

Wine grapes grow best between the 30 and 50 latitudes north and south, but the influence of ocean currents on temperature allows some regions outside these latitudinal bands to grow grapes. Wine-producing regions generally fall in a band with average temperatures between 10 and 20 degrees Celsius.

# THE TOP TEN WINE-PRODUCING COUNTRIES IN THE WORLD

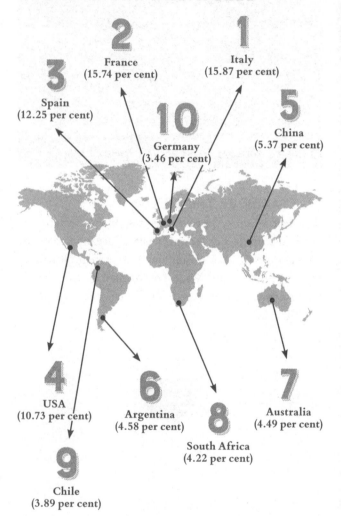

**2**
France
(15.74 per cent)

**1**
Italy
(15.87 per cent)

**3**
Spain
(12.25 per cent)

**5**
China
(5.37 per cent)

**10**
Germany
(3.46 per cent)

**4**
USA
(10.73 per cent)

**6**
Argentina
(4.58 per cent)

**8**
South Africa
(4.22 per cent)

**7**
Australia
(4.49 per cent)

**9**
Chile
(3.89 per cent)

Source of statistics: www.wineinstitute.org

## WHICH COUNTRY IS THE BIGGEST WINE PRODUCER?

The order of the top three wine-producing countries is different depending on the statistics consulted: whether it is all grapes including non-wine grapes, whether it is in litres produced or in hectares planted. If consulting gross vineyard acreage, Spain is top followed by France then Italy. The latest statistics for wine volume put Italy first in litres produced, followed by France then Spain. But according to an Australian academic study, the largest hectarage of wine-grape production in 2010 was in France and its hectarage grew between 2000 and 2010 despite the wine crisis created by too much supply relative to demand. In 2013, global wine production was around 278 million hectolitres while consumption was around 238 million hectolitres. It's a buyer's market.

# WHO IS DRINKING ALL THIS WINE?

Despite the low per capita wine consumption, China is the world's biggest wine-consuming country, thanks to its large population: 155 million 9-litre (12-bottle) cases in 2013, compared to the French who came in at 150 million 9-litre cases that year.

CHINA
1 Litre per capita

USA
10 Litres per capita

UK
20 Litres per capita

**FRANCE**
44 Litres per capita

**ANDORRA**
46 Litres per capita

**VATICAN CITY**
74 Litres per capita

# WHAT'S IN A BOTTLE?

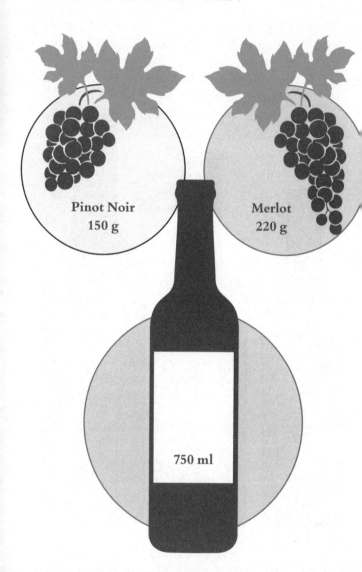

Pinot Noir
150 g

Merlot
220 g

750 ml

A 750-ml bottle of average-sized grapes will contain about 500 grapes. The weight of the grape and the bunch depends on the grape type and the season; more water means bigger and heavier grapes versus smaller and lighter grapes in a drought. A typical bunch of Pinot Noir weighs around 150 g, significantly less than a bunch of Merlot at around 220 g. A single healthy high-volume Merlot vine with twelve bunches can produce around two bottles.

## COULD YOU TRY EVERY WINE IN YOUR LIFETIME?

There are so many wines out there, it is impossible to get to them all… If you drink a glass from a different wine every day for all of your adult life, you will try around 20,000 bottles. In the Bordeaux region of France alone, there are more than 60 *appellations* and about 10,000 châteaux or named vineyards, even more reason to use the technique of wine tasting to be sure that you drink the best quality and match of wine for your palate. The variety of *terroirs* is part of the explanation for the explosion of wine *appellations*. The *appellation* system is supposed to help you know what you are buying and drinking, but in fact there are so many *appellations* that it is hard to know what is going on even if you are a master in wine.

## THE MAJOR WINE REGIONS OF THE WORLD

The best-known wine regions can be found in France, Italy, Spain and Germany (the Old World) and in California, Australia, New Zealand, South Africa, Argentina and Chile (the New World). China is a big player in terms of production figures but is not recognised for fine wines… yet. It has been importing know-how from France and other leading wine producers and will likely surprise us with the quality and value of its wines in a few years.

# GEOGRAPHICAL AND QUALITY CLASSIFICATIONS

Europe is a web of geographical and quality classifications that could have even the most expert wine buff confused. But a little knowledge of these things can help your wine-selection confidence in a big way.

## *APPELLATION*, PDO, AOP, AOC, DOC AND AVA: TLAS GONE MAD

Before I entered the world of wine production, I thought the world of technology was the king of TLAs, three letter acronyms; now I know it is the world of wine. The French word *appellation* means 'name'. When we use it in the context of wine it is a shortening of the words *appellation d'origine contrôlée* (AOC), the traditional French name for an EU category called PDO (Protected Designation of Origin). The official EU name for this PDO category is AOP (*appellation d'origine protégée*) in French. In Italy and Portugal the PDO used to be (and still can be) called DOC; and in Spain, DO. Essentially these mean a protected area of origin with strict and controlled rules of production. A few parts of the New World have started to move in this direction but they are much less regulated. In the USA the AVA or American Viticultural Area now defines and protects places like Napa but does not regulate exactly what producers can and can't do in quite the same way that PDO does in Europe.

**Confused? I'm not surprised.
This handy list of the different
European terms for PDO should help.**

**Protected Designation of
Origin Terms in Europe**

### France
*Appellation d'origine protégée* (AOP)
was and can still be called AOC

### Spain
*Denominación de origen protegida* (DOP)
was and can still be called DO

### Italy
*Denominazione di origine protetta* (DOP)
was and can still be called DOC

### Germany
*Geschützte Ursprungsbezeichnung* (g.U.)

### Portugal
*Denominaçaõ de origem protegida* (DOP)
was and can still be called DOC

### Hungary
*Oltalom alatt álló eredetmegjelölés* (OEM)

## THE MEANING OF 'CHÂTEAU'

'Château' is a term used in France for a wine estate that makes and bottles their own wine on the property. Directly translated, it means 'castle', but only a tiny percentage of properties using this denomination actually have a castle. It can only be used if the producer grows the grapes, makes the wine and bottles it at the estate as well as meeting the *appellation* rules.

### DECIPHERING A WINE LABEL: IS IT A BULK WINE OR AN ARTISAN WINE?

Take a look at the wine labels in your local wine shop. See if you can pick out the wines that have been made and bottled by an individual winemaker versus those that are bulk wine bottled by a merchant. On French wine labels the term *Mis en bouteille au château/domaine* means 'grown and bottled at the estate'. In the New World this is equivalent to 'Estate grown and bottled'.

There are many famous estates with home farms that produce estate-bottled wine but then also produce mass brand wines under the same name that are not estate grown and bottled. Like so many products today, it pays to read the fine print or to find a specialist wine shop that you trust to do that on your behalf.

## *VIN DE PAYS*, PGI AND IGP

Alongside the PDO system is PGI (Protected Geographical Indication). This is the *Vin de Pays* or *L'indication géographique protégée* (IGP) in France, and what used to be called *Indicazione geografica tipica* in Italy, *Vino de la Tierra* in Spain, and *Landwein* in Germany and Austria. It is controlled in a similar way to PDO (AOC) but with lighter production rules e.g. *Appellation Bordeaux* red wines have a maximum yield of around 6,700 litres per hectare while the maximum yield for *Vin de Pays de l'Atlantique* is closer to 10,000 litres per hectare. Considering this aspect of production alone, it is easy to understand that a *Vin de Pays d'Oc* is on average likely to be less expensive than an AOC like a Corbières in the same region.

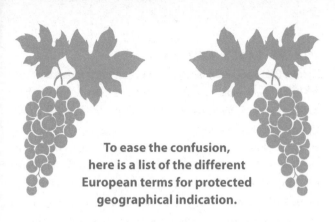

**To ease the confusion,
here is a list of the different
European terms for protected
geographical indication.**

**Protected Geographical Indication Terms in Europe**

**France**
*Indication géographique protégée* (IGP), was
and still can be called *Vin de Pays*

**Spain**
*Indicación geográfica protegida* (IGP), was
and still can be called *Vino de la Tierra*

**Italy**
*Indicazione geografica protetta* (IGP), was and still
can be called *Indicazione geografica tipica*

**Germany**
*Geschützte geographische Angabe* (g.g.A),
was and still can be called *Landwein*

**Portugal**
*Indicações geográficas protegidas* (IGP)

**Hungary**
*Oltalom alatt álló földrajzi jelzések* (OFJ)

## *VIN DE TABLE* AND VSIG

Below PDO and PGI is the 'no geographical indication' or VSIG (*Vin sans indication géographique*). In French this is what used to be *vin de table*, table wine in English or *vino da tavola* in Italian. This has no quality control save the general EU rules for wine. This sounds like it must be the bottom of the rung – and it can be – but you can also find an excellent premium wine labelled VSIG or *Vin de Table*. This is true for many reasons. More and more quality artisanal and natural *vignerons* (winegrowers) are choosing to go off the *appellation* system and are making wines that are unique and of high quality but that don't fit the straitjacket of the PGI or PDO. A wine can be excluded from the PDO for a wrong grape (even if it is a heritage grape), a slightly different colour or a different style to the norm in the region.

### WHAT'S IN A COLOUR? A GREAT ILLUSTRATION OF PDO GONE WRONG

In PDO Bergerac rosé, the colour of rosé is set within a specific set of tones that are 'medium plus' coloured. Since the original setting of these rules, wine lovers have clearly voted for pale rosé. They consider it better quality and expect to pay more than for a darker rosé. The Bergerac producers that make their wine in this paler style meet their customers' demands but lose their *appellation* status, suggesting that the traditional products that the PDOs (AOCs in France) protect may be stuck in a rut rather than evolving with the market.

## MORE ON THE PDO

The PDO system has its roots in the 1500s, when an early version of PDO was given to Roquefort cheese. Now it is a many-tentacled monster that is rigorously controlled. In France every AOC wine has been scientifically analysed for faults and most have been tasted by a panel of judges to see if they meet the required quality standards. Some wines may pass these stringent tests then be downgraded after bottling through a tainted cork, bad storage or bad bottling conditions. The more transparent the wine-supply chain, the safer you are. If you buy direct from the producer, you can be surer of the wine than if you buy a wine that has passed from grape producer to winemaker to merchant to importer to distributor and then finally to your local shop.

### It's complicated but it can be helpful

The PDO (or AOC in France) system for wines can be complicated, inconsistent, close to incomprehensible and, as explained above, it is also not the only quality wine. The INAO (Institut national de l'origine et de la qualité) of France recognises more than 300 wine *appellations*. Add to that all the Italian, Spanish, German, Portuguese and New World vineyards and you'd be set to go mad. Don't despair. Start with a grape or area you know you like, then explore similar areas and flavours, constantly spreading your wings and experimenting from there. Despite all its constraints, with a little nurturing PDO can become a friend to aid your wine choices.

## PRODUCTION RULES, RIGHT DOWN TO THE NUMBER OF BUDS PER VINE

Each *appellation* has a different set of production rules and standards, making it complex even for wine specialists and for the producers themselves. The rules are prescribed and enforced down to such fine details as the number of buds per vine in certain *appellations*. Each *appellation* strictly prescribes the varietals that can be used, so if you know the *appellation* you can find out the most likely varietals in the wine even if they are not on the label.

## GENERIC TO REGION TO COMMUNE

Within a PDO we can find more PDOs – they're like the many layers of a Russian doll.

Within one enormous wine area like Bordeaux we find regional *appellations* like the Médoc, and then within that we find further *appellations* at the *commune* level, like Margaux and Pauillac.

District (or *commune*) *appellations* can offer real *terroir* nuances, such as:

- **St-Emilion:** The most recognised commune wine *appellation* in the world, home to some of the most expensive wines, like Ausone and Cheval Blanc. The soil is mostly limestone and clay. Typically the blend is majority Merlot, offering smooth, generous and accessible wines.

- **Pauillac:** A commune within the *appellation* of Haut-Médoc, home to three of the five red wines classified *premier grand cru classé* as long ago as 1855. A gravel layer and slightly warmer conditions than St-Emilion mean this blend is generally biased towards Cabernet Sauvignon, offering tannic wines with longevity and classic blackcurrant aromas.

In the past, French producers just had the *appellation* and didn't mention the grape varietals on the label. Now many do, and this makes life easier for wine lovers. If we take Bordeaux reds, for example, most of these wines are primarily a blend of Merlot and Cabernet Sauvignon.

Irrigation is illegal for vines producing wine within AOCS in France (it is legal to water baby vines that are not producing fruit yet). The amount of water that arrives thanks to nature is seen as part of the *terroir* and part of the taste, hence the producer is not allowed to alter it.

# SEVERAL WELL-KNOWN OLD WORLD REGIONS AND GRAPE VARIETIES, AND THEIR NEW WORLD RIVALS

| Old World Wine Region | Grape Varieties | New World Competitors |
| --- | --- | --- |
| Bordeaux and Bergerac reds (France) | Merlot, Cabernet Sauvignon, Cabernet Franc, Malbec | Australia, South Africa, 'Meritage' blends in the USA |
| Bordeaux and Bergerac whites (France) | Sémillon, Sauvignon Blanc | New Zealand, Australia, South Africa, Chile |
| Burgundy reds (France) | Pinot Noir (also Gamay in the south for Beaujolais) | USA (Oregon), New Zealand, Australia, South Africa |
| Burgundy whites (France) | Chardonnay (also Aligoté in some parts) | Australia, USA, South Africa |
| Northern Rhône reds (France) | Syrah (Shiraz) | Australia, USA, South Africa |
| Northern Rhône whites (France) | Viognier, Roussanne and Marsanne | California |

| Old World Wine Region | Grape Varieties | New World Competitors |
|---|---|---|
| Southern Rhône reds (France) | Syrah (Shiraz), Grenache, Cinsault, Mourvèdre | Australia, USA, South Africa |
| Alsace (France/ Germany) | Gewürztraminer, Riesling | New Zealand, Australia, USA |
| Loire Valley reds (France) | Cabernet Franc, some Gamay and Malbec | California has begun planting Cabernet Franc, Argentina for Malbec |
| Loire Valley whites (France) | Chenin Blanc in *commune appellation* wines like Savennières, Vouvray | South Africa |
| Loire Valley whites (France) | Sauvignon Blanc *commune appellation* wines, including Sancerre, Pouilly-Fumé | New Zealand, Chile, South Africa |
| Champagne The other Old World sparkling that is *méthode traditionelle* (MT) is Cava (Spain) | Chardonnay, Pinot Noir, Pinot Meunier | USA, Australia, New Zealand, South Africa (Cap Classique) |

| Old World Wine Region | Grape Varieties | New World Competitors |
|---|---|---|
| Rioja (Spain) | Tempranillo, Garnacha (Grenache), Mazuelo (Carignan) | Argentina, Australia, California |
| Barolo (Italy) | Nebbiolo | Some planting in Australia and USA |
| Chianti (Italy) | Sangiovese | Some planting in Australia and USA |

## THE *GRAND CRU* CONCEPT

A *grand cru* is a regional wine classification designating a vineyard with a history and a reputation for producing great wines. It is usually the classification of a vineyard's quality potential rather than the actual quality of individual wines. However, the *grand cru* concept has been applied differently across the four main regions in France where we find them, namely Bordeaux, Burgundy, Alsace and Champagne.

## THE FIRST *GRANDS CRUS*

The idea of *grand cru* is ancient, as there is proof that the Romans classified their best vineyards more than two millennia ago.

Bordeaux is the most famous of the *grands crus* because of the well-publicised 1855 classification of the Left Bank vineyards requested by Napoleon III. In St-Emilion, on the Right Bank, *grands crus* were put in place 100 years later in a different format.

Burgundy is thought to have been the first to apply the concept of *grand cru* in France back in medieval times, but it was only formalised there in 1861. Champagne and Alsace eventually followed in 1950 and 1975 respectively.

## BORDEAUX *GRANDS CRUS* VERSUS
## BURGUNDY *GRANDS CRUS*

The *grand cru* classification of the Left Bank of the Bordeaux *appellation* in 1855 classified the best red wines of the Médoc (plus one outsider) and the top dessert wines of Sauternes and Barsac. St-Emilion winegrowers on the Right Bank, also renowned for their quality, realised it was a great idea but took 100 years to introduce their classification.

The major difference between the two systems is that the 1855 classification was cast in stone, never to be reviewed save for one exception (the upgrading of Mouton Rothschild from second to first class in 1973), while the St-Emilion classification is reviewed every ten years.

What sets the Bordeaux classifications apart from that of Burgundy (and the others) is that it is the château (the wine business with its associated vineyards) that is classified rather than the exact borders of the physical vineyard. This means that the property can add vineyard land to its holdings, within reason, and they will still be *grand cru classé*. By the same score, classified vineyards can be sold to another entity and thereby lose their classification, as was the case with some vineyards now owned by Château Gloria in St Julien.

In Burgundy, the land has the status and it can be divided into many pieces and still keep that status so, for example, Clos de Vougeot, a *grand cru* of about 50 hectares (125 acres) has around 80 different owners. The label may look the same, but if you look at the fine print of the producer you will find very different qualities even on this single *grand cru* vineyard.

The 1855 Médoc classification was based primarily on prices achieved by châteaux in the years running up to 1855 and categorised them into five levels from *Premier Grand Cru Classé* at the top to *Cinquième Grand Cru Classé*. Many ask if a classification carried out more than 150 years ago is still relevant today. They have a point. In some instances it is almost turned upside down with some fifth-level *grands crus classés* (e.g. Pontet-Canet) achieving prices higher than many second-level *grands crus classés*. But regular reviews of classifications cause their own problems, as was seen in the highly publicised court case about the St-Emilion 2006 classification review. Retail prices for *grands crus classés* from Médoc start at around €25 for a *cinquième grand cru classé* and run to thousands of euros for a *premier grand cru classé* from a top vintage.

## 'SECOND WINES'

There can be great value in 'second wines' from the top estates. Second wines are normally taken from younger parcels – vines that are under 15 years old – and are sometimes almost as good quality as the first, but much less expensive. Their names are usually easy to recognise as they carry the grand estate's name along with some modifying words. Examples include: Carruades de Lafite, Petit Mouton de Mouton Rothschild, Pavillon Rouge du Château Margaux, Les Forts de Latour, Les Pagodes de Cos, Les Charmes de Kirwan and Les Hauts de Pontet-Canet.

## BILLIONAIRE'S VINEGAR AND 'THOU SHALT NOT SELL FAKE WINE'

The value of the top wines of the world means that they are regular targets of fraudsters looking to make a quick buck. *The Billionaire's Vinegar* by Benjamin Wallace is a great exposé of one of the biggest wine frauds in history. Rudy Kurniawan is the main culprit in this page-turning true story about wine fraud on a grand scale.

Human history has a habit of repeating itself. A well-preserved Babylonian legal code of Ancient Mesopotamia, dating to about 1754 BC and known as the Code of Hammurabi, is one of the world's most ancient deciphered writings. It consists of 282 laws, one of which states that anyone caught selling fraudulent wine should be drowned in a river.

Luckily for Rudy, we have moved on from death by drowning for wine fraud and he was merely given ten years in prison and ordered to make a massive repayment (around 28 million US dollars) to his victims. You can see the ancient code for yourself in the Louvre Museum in Paris; it is written on a large black stone that is more than two metres high and in the shape of an index finger.

# WINEGROWING METHODS

Winegrowing or viticulture, like most agriculture, has become mechanised and industrialised over the last century. But no matter how mechanised we may try to make it, today viticulture is still one of the most labour-intensive types of agriculture. In an effort to reduce this dependence on labour, viticulture found chemical solutions to some of its problems, such as herbicides to remove weeds and chemical fertilisers to increase volume, which ironically have led to more disease and therefore the need for yet more pesticides and fungicides. As long as there have been agricultural chemicals for sale, however, there have also been those who have rejected them.

## WHY SHOULD YOU CARE ABOUT HOW YOUR WINE IS GROWN?

Here are four top reasons to choose wine made from organically grown grapes:

- **Your health:** Conventionally farmed grapes have been found to contain high levels of pesticide residues. Some of these systemic chemicals are highly carcinogenic; others can disrupt the nervous or reproductive systems.

- **The health of farmers and workers**: The health of the people working in the vineyard is directly impacted by chemical farming. Studies have linked high levels of cancer among vineyard workers in the US with vineyard pesticides. France officially recognised cancer from exposure to pesticides as a work-related illness in 2015.

**The health of the land**: Extensive erosion (from herbicides), toxic salinity in the soil (from chemical fertilisers and irrigation) and lack of biodiversity (from pesticides and herbicides) are the results of conventional chemical-dependent farming. At the most basic level, the poisons end up in the water supply of the region the wine is grown in.

**The taste**: Recent studies have found that polyphenolic substances (the natural flavour compounds found in wine) and antioxidants (which fight cancer) are higher in organic wines than in conventional wines. The most expensive wine in the world, Romanée-Conti from Burgundy, is certified organic and biodynamic.

## FOUR KEY TYPES OF VITICULTURE

There are four main categories of viticulture that can be easily defined:

## 1. CONVENTIONAL VITICULTURE

In conventional viticulture a winegrower will use chemical fertiliser to increase production, herbicide to kill plant competition, systemic pesticides to kill insects and systemic fungicides to combat fungal disease like mildew. At worst, a conventional farmer will use the maximum recommended dose of everything, which makes the vine weak. It is like humans taking antibiotics 24/7, just in case.

## 2. REASONED CHEMICAL VITICULTURE

This is often called 'sustainable viticulture' (*lutte raisonnée* in French). The farmer can use the chemicals listed above but they must consider other options and check the vineyard, for example counting the pests to assess whether pesticide is necessary and how much is required, rather than spraying a systemic insecticide by rote. But like the word 'natural', the all-pervasive and uncontrolled use of the word 'sustainable' today has rendered it largely meaningless at times.

## 3. ORGANIC VITICULTURE

'Organic' is a certified term that guarantees that what you are buying has been farmed without chemical fertilisers and without the 'icides' (herbicides and systemic pesticides and fungicides). For wine in Europe, the organic rules go beyond the farming into the winemaking (see Chapter 4).

## 4. BIODYNAMIC VITICULTURE

To be biodynamic, the farm must already be certified organic and then go a step further, trying to understand the farm in its environment and creating a biodiverse (many different kinds of plants, animals, insects) farm. Put simply, biodynamics is three things: thinking of the farm as a whole farm system; working in harmony with the calendar of the earth's movements in relation to the moon, planets and constellations (think of the effect of the moon on the tides and then imagine its effect on the water content and flow in a plant); and using plant- and animal-based homeopathic-type preparations to aid plants to grow and protect themselves.

A recent study found the average pesticide levels in 92 wines bought randomly off the shelf to be more than 300 times what is allowed in our water supply.

The analysis was financed and published by a consumer watchdog magazine in France. The only way to be sure you are not drinking wine with pesticide residues is to buy certified organic wine.

## WORK IN THE VINEYARD THROUGH THE SEASONS (NORTHERN HEMISPHERE)

Usually bud break is around April, flowering is in June, and harvest is late August to early October. The seasons and key activities are the same between conventional and organic; it is the method that changes – for example, herbicide for the removal of weeds in conventional viticulture and mechanical weeding (hoeing, ploughing or mowing) in organic.

### Conventional viticulture

- November: vineyard maintenance and chemical fertilisers
- December–March: pruning
- April–July: chemical herbicide, systemic chemical fungicides, chemical shoot shrivelling, chemical insecticides and vine trimming
- August: maintenance and winery preparation
- September–October: harvest and winemaking

### Organic viticulture

- November: vineyard maintenance and building soil fertility; covering crops and natural composting
- December–March: pruning
- April: initial mechanical weeding, close observation

- May–July: mechanical weeding, mowing, mechanical or hand shoot-removal, application of contact antifungals, vine trimming if necessary

- August: maintenance and winery preparation

- September–October: harvest and winemaking

## CONCLUSION

Winegrowing is 90 per cent of the end product. It is impossible to make great wine with bad grapes. However, it is possible to make bad wine with good grapes and to make bad grapes look good with fancy footwork in the winery. A passionate winegrower will take you into their vines, not their winery. You will see the love they have for the living vines and their magical transformation of sunlight and water into the potential to make wine.

## CHAPTER 4

# WINEMAKING AND ITS EFFECT ON THE END PRODUCT

### 'MAKING GOOD WINE IS A SKILL. FINE WINE IS AN ART.'

#### ROBERT MONDAVI

. . . . . . . . . . . . . . . . . . . . . . . . . . . . . . . . . . . . . . . . . . . . . .

We all conjure up images of beautiful barrels and peaceful, quiet cellars when we think of winemaking. Yes, there are moments like this in a wine's life, but most winemaking is hard work, involving serious physical labour, attention to detail, skill and art.

## THE PROCESS OF WINEMAKING

Wine is fermented grape juice. In its simplest form, winemaking is picking grapes, pressing them, moving the pressed juice (white or rosé) or whole grapes (reds) into a vat and letting the yeast have some fun fermenting the content, converting the sugar to alcohol in the process. Voilà! The wine can be finished and ready to bottle in less than ten days or as much as five years. Of course, a lot can go wrong along the way; if you leave the grapes and hope for the best, they could go the way of vinegar, hence the importance of the winemaker and their know-how.

# BASIC WINEMAKING STEPS

## WHITE WINE & ROSÉ

PICK

↓

PRESS

↓

FERMENT

↓

MATURE

## RED WINE

PICK

↓

FERMENT
(ON THE GRAPES' SKIN)

↓

PRESS

↓

MATURE

## EXPERIENCE AND ADAPTABILITY

Each step in winemaking is complex and the way in which each step is undertaken can have a dramatic impact on the wine. The temperature involved in each step must be considered, the speed of fermentation, the clarity of white wine, the texture of the cap for red wine, the smell of the wine. During the winemaking season (from September to November in the northern hemisphere) most wineries are like baby wards: each morning and evening the progress of the wines is checked, their temperatures are taken, their aromas are checked and thinking about next steps begins. Anyone can find a wine recipe online, but what makes the difference is the experience of the winemaker with their *terroir* and their wine.

## PICKING THE GRAPES

There are two key decisions at the start of the winemaking process: when to pick and how to pick. The when to pick depends on the style of wine the grower wants to make and the season's conditions. The growers walk the vineyards tasting the skins, pips and pulp, assessing the ripeness and balance between the sugar, acid and tannin in order to decide the best moment to harvest. They also analyse the grapes for the scientific levels of these elements, but in the end our tastebuds are the best judge.

**Hand-picking versus machine picking**

Machine picking is less expensive, particularly in countries with expensive labour like France. Despite this, all the best vineyards hand-pick because hand-picking enables better sorting. For the moment, even the most sophisticated machine harvester cannot select the grapes as well as a trained and motivated person.

## HAND-PICKING TO AVOID CRITTER COLLATERAL

For wines that are truly vegan (that don't use animal products in winemaking), hand harvesting is necessary since machine-harvested grapes include many small animals: mice, lizards, snakes and even entire rabbits. For red, you find out what was in your 'blend' when you dig the skins out at the end of the winemaking. One ton of grapes, half a snake, one lizard, two mice, three quarters of a frog... It sounds like a witch's brew, not a recipe for good wine.

### Hand-picking and sulphur dioxide or sulphites

Hand-picking can reduce the level of sulphites, the preservative used in winemaking. When the grapes are picked with care and skins remain closed, there is no oxidation, hence no need for sulphites. Once the grapes are in the winery they can be protected with inert gas like nitrogen. Sulphites cause inflammation so for your health and your head it is better if they are lower rather than higher.

### More benefits of hand-picking

Hand-picking is also about positive energy, the community and attention to detail. After a farmer has taken so much care throughout the growing season, to start the grapes' journey into wine with violent thrashing through the vineyard by a three-ton machine doesn't make sense. With a good team, there is also a great camaraderie to hand-picking, even on back-breaking long days. There is a sense of community, of working together and of excitement.

## PRESSING THE GRAPES

For white and rosé wine the grapes are pressed before fermenting and for red after. For the white the just-picked grapes are pressed gently in order to garner as much grape juice as possible without releasing the bitter oils from the seeds. It is a fine balance. The leftover skins and seeds are composted or given to a distillery to make industrial alcohol. For red wine the colour and tannin comes from contact with the skins during the fermentation process. At the end of the process the free wine is run out of the tank and the skins are then dug out and pressed. This gives a further 10–20 per cent of wine called 'press wine'. It is usually more tannic and rustic than the free run wine.

### NAPOLEON'S THIRSTY SOLDIERS

French winegrowers have to give 1 per cent of their crop to the state – an ancient tax created by Napoleon as a way to provide wine for his troops. Taxes rarely disappear so, while this wine does not go to the French army today, producers still have to provide the equivalent in lees wine and grape must (skins, pips and pulp) left after pressing to state distilleries, who turn them into industrial alcohol for medicinal or cosmetic purposes.

### White wine from red grapes

Most red grapes have white juice; the colour is in the skins. To make red wine the skins must stay with the juice for a good few days or even a month for a powerful style of wine. To make rosé wine the skins can be kept with the juice for a couple of hours. You can make white wine from red grapes and this is called *blanc de noir* ('white from black').

## THE FERMENTATION PROCESS

We allow the grapes (for red) or the juice (for white) to increase in temperature so that the fermentation can start. This is either natural or by added yeast. The yeast then eats the sugar and transforms it into alcohol and carbon dioxide, also giving off much-needed heat in the process.

### Cultured yeast versus wild indigenous yeast

In most wine today a cultured yeast created in a factory starts the fermentation, but this is not strictly necessary. There are wild yeasts on the grape skins that offer the unique flavours of their place. For this reason most natural winemakers don't add yeast; they let the grapes do the fermentation naturally, with their own indigenous yeast. It is possible to buy cultured yeasts created to give a specific flavour to your wine, such as pineapple or banana. When you have a wine with a single, very powerful aroma, this may be the reason: it could be a manufactured aroma.

## Killer gas

Many winemakers have died of $CO_2$ asphyxiation so being aware of this danger and ensuring the winery has good ventilation is of prime importance.

### A 'NEW' WINEMAKER VERSUS AN 'OLD' WINEMAKER: SHOULD WINERIES CHANGE THEIR WINEMAKER AS OFTEN AS THEY CHANGE THEIR UNDERPANTS?

New World wineries release 'hot news' about appointing new winemakers and this is quite at odds with the approach in much of the Old World. In the New World, new winemakers and a technical approach are celebrated, while in the Old World winemaking remains more traditional and a winemaker's knowledge of *terroir* and viticulture is crucial. For example, at Château Haut-Brion, a *premier grand cru classé* in Bordeaux, the Delmas family has managed the estate, both the winegrowing and the winemaking, for the owners for three generations.

## Malolactic fermentation or 'malo'

'Malo' is shorthand for malolactic fermentation, a natural deacidification that takes place in most red wines. It is a conversion of malic acid (like green-apple acid) to lactic acid (like milk acid), which makes the wine smoother. It usually happens naturally during the summer following harvest, as soon as temperatures rise again, although it is possible to encourage this process to take place in winter with heat and lactic bacteria. In general, white wine has not done the 'malo' and red wine has, but there are exceptions. A big buttery Chardonnay that has low acid and a creamy buttery note probably has done the malo while a fresh and zesty Beaujolais Nouveau red has not.

## Methods of extraction

With red wine the entire grape is placed in the fermentation vat rather than just the juice, as is the case with most white and rosé. The skins rise to the top, making a clear cap on top of the juice (extracted naturally by the weight of the grapes or by a light crushing, not pressing). Since they are separated and the colour is in the skins, we need to get the juice in contact with them to extract the colour and the tannins. To do this the winemaker has two options: to pump the juice over the top like a coffee percolator or to push the cap of skins back down into the juice like a French press coffee pot. This is usually done two or three times a day. For pump-overs the volume and number depends on how much extraction is sought. This extraction process continues through the fermentation period and sometimes even longer, when it is known as 'post-fermentation maceration'.

## TWO WAYS TO MAKE ROSÉ

Rosé can be made by pressing red grapes picked exclusively to make rosé or by the *saignée* or 'bleeding' method. With the *saignée* method, 10 to 15 per cent of the juice from a vat of red grapes destined for red wine is run off about 12 hours after picking. This makes the red that is left more concentrated (more skin to juice than before the *saignée*) and gives a by-product of rosé wine. This is usually a darker-coloured and higher-alcohol style rosé (it was picked to be red wine after all) typical of Bordeaux and Bergerac, while a rosé made by the press method is paler and fresher and tends to be more typical in Provence.

## THE MATURING AND BOTTLING PROCESS

A simple wine might be bottled to be drunk immediately, while a more complex wine might be barrel-aged, bottled much later and able to age further in the bottle.

# HOW MANY BOTTLES IN THAT BARREL? HOW MANY POTENTIAL BOTTLES IN THAT VINEYARD?

A standard bottle contains 750 ml

A Bordeaux barrel contains 225 litres or 300 bottles worth of wine

A pallet contains 450 litres or 600 bottles worth of wine

A vineyard of one acre is able to produce one to ten pallets of wine, averaging around five pallets

### Cork versus screwcap

This is a complex question. Cork is a great closure but with a *grande bête noire*: cork taint, a bacteria in the cork that can change the aromas of your favourite wine from fruit to wet dog or damp basement – not what you want to drink. From an ecological standpoint, real cork is better as it is a renewable resource. From a health standpoint, having your wine in contact with cork is better than having it in contact with the plastic liner of a screwcap, which can leach plastic components into the wine. For long-term storage, cork wins based on this factor alone.

Screwcap has been gaining ground on traditional cork for many years, approximately doubling in France and Germany between 2008 and 2013. The UK screwcap was already significant but also grew its market share over those five years, partly due to supermarket buyers demanding it from suppliers to avoid the cork taint problem.

# WINEMAKING AND ITS EFFECT ON THE END PRODUCT

# CORK VERSUS SCREWCAP

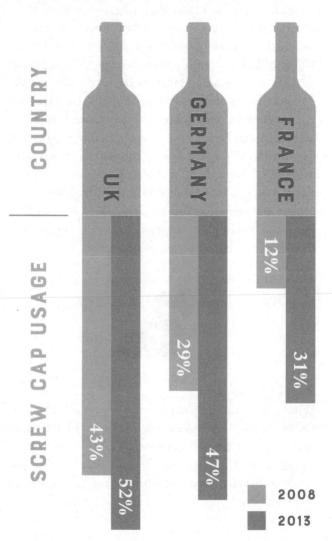

**COUNTRY**

UK

GERMANY

FRANCE

**SCREW CAP USAGE**

France: 12%, 31%

Germany: 29%, 47%

UK: 43%, 52%

2008
2013

## Light damage and clear bottles

Wine drinkers have said they like to see what is in the bottle so supermarkets often force growers to choose clear bottles, especially for white and rosé. Unfortunately, like oil, wine is damaged and degraded by light so a coloured bottle is far better for storage. The polyphenols (aroma compounds) can change; citrus aromas decrease and cooked cabbage aromas increase… definitely not what we want. Vitamins are also degraded by UV light and wine can include vitamins B2 (riboflavin), B6 and B12 and trace levels of A, C and K along with other useful minerals like manganese, zinc, copper and selenium. Brown glass is best, followed by green and, in last place, the least effective for protecting the wine from light damage, is clear glass.

## Deposits in your wine

Wine made naturally often throws a deposit at the bottom of the bottle. Sometimes you can even find tartrate crystals on the inside of your cork. This is perfectly fine, and in fact better for you and for your wine. A wine that has been heavily fined and filtered may be beautifully clear with no deposit but will have lost a part of its soul along the way.

# DIFFERENT WINEMAKING METHODS AND WINE STYLES

With exactly the same winemaking steps, we can get completely different wines in the end, for example through different times of harvest, different maturation, second fermentation or malolactic fermentation.

## ORGANIC, BIODYNAMIC AND NATURAL WINEMAKING

Organic wine rules came into effect in the EU from vintage 2012 onwards. All wines with the European organic leaf logo now mean guaranteed organic winemaking and not just organic viticulture. One of the most important differences for wine lovers is that you are guaranteed lower sulphites. Many other intrants (products added to the grapes or juice during the winemaking process) allowed in conventional wines are not allowed in organic so overall you are also guaranteed a purer wine with fewer additives. While the underlying farming method remains the most important reason for seeking out the organic label, the addition of winemaking rules is clearly also good news for wine lovers as a guarantee of quality. But organic producers pay more for certification as the growing and the winemaking are controlled and guaranteed. In addition, winemakers need to have more rigorous processes in place to be able to meet the legislated lower sulphites.

## ORGANIC WINE AND LOWER SULPHITES

The new organic wine rules mean lower sulphites. To take a concrete example for red wine, the EU norm is 150 mg/litre, the new organic wine rule is 100 mg/litre and the biodynamic Demeter (the largest international certification body in biodynamics) rule is 70 mg/litre.

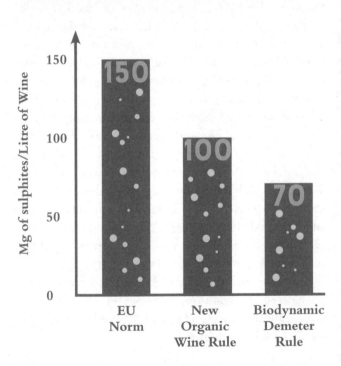

## WHY SHOULD YOU CARE ABOUT SULPHITES?

If you like your wine, you could be taking in far more sulphites than is recommended by the WHO (World Health Organization). They recommend a maximum of 0.7 mg per kg of body weight per day. So a person weighing 75 kg should have about 52 mg per day. At EU-legislated maximum levels for dry white wine that would be a third of a bottle per day, but wine isn't the only product with sulphites in it. Some countries have higher legislated maximum levels for wine than the EU. For example, the USA has a legislated limit across all wines of 350 mg/litre (more than double the EU level for conventional red wines and three times the level for organic wines). At this level you would be at the recommended WHO limit with one small glass of wine.

## 'NO SULPHITES ADDED' AND NATURAL WINES

Natural wines have no or very little sulphite added but, while there are more natural wines on the market than ever, there is no certification that includes this term. Some natural wines and no-sulphite-added wines are funky and very different and some are closer to what you expect in a more traditional wine but with less of a hangover if you overindulge. If you are keen on buying natural wines, talk to your wine specialist about the styles you like and which of these might suit your tastes best.

## EARLY HARVEST VERSUS LATE HARVEST

When we pick has an impact on the style of the wine. In simplest terms, grapes picked early in harvest season have less sugar and more acid, while grapes picked late have more sugar and less acid.

## SIMPLE TANK-AGEING VERSUS BARREL-AGEING

A wine that is matured for a short time in a tank will retain its fresh-fruit characteristics. A wine aged for longer in a barrel will display aged characteristics like cooked fruit and earthy notes and barrel characteristics like toast, vanilla and sweet spice.

## FACTORY VERSUS ARTISANAL WINEMAKING

There are two styles of winemaking: one where the winery wants to create a standardised product, along the lines of a cola, that doesn't change with the vintage; and another where the vintage differences are embraced and the wines are made to be different each year according to the growing conditions. With the first style, technology and additives are used to ensure the wine is the same, so if the grape juice is short of sugar then sugar is added, or if the wine is short of acid then acid is added (this can be any food-grade acid rather than natural grape acid). With the second style, there can be noticeable vintage differences and the wine's character remains true to its vintage.

## SWEET OR DESSERT WINES

There are three main categories of sweet wine:

1. **FORTIFIED WINE:** Late-harvested grapes are partially fermented then fortified with distilled spirit (usually brandy, i.e. a spirit distilled from grape wine), thereby raising the alcohol to a higher level (around 15–18 per cent). This stops the fermentation and keeps the residual sugar as sweetness. Two of the most famous are Port and Muscat de Baumes de Venise.

2. **NOBLE ROT WINE:** Late in the season with the right conditions – misty mornings and sunny afternoons – grapes are attacked by the *Botrytis cinerea* fungus (after the Latin for 'ash', because it looks like a fine dusting of ash), which makes tiny holes in the skins of the grapes. The miracle of this particular rot is that it allows water to escape without letting bacteria in, rather like the pores of our skin allowing sweat to escape but not allowing bacteria in. This concentration of sugar means that the grapes are so sweet when picked that, even after fermenting to around 12 per cent alcohol, there is still enough sugar left to make the wine sweet (50–150g/l,

equivalent to 10–30 teaspoons per litre). The most famous example is Sauternes in the Bordeaux region. Botrytis wines usually offer notes of apricot compote, honey and almond in their youth, and notes of marmalade, caramel and grilled nuts with age.

3. **ICE WINE:** It is the freezing of the grapes still on the vines that creates the extra sweetness. The grapes are picked in extremely cold conditions, usually at least −10 degrees Celcius, then pressed immediately, and the ice that floats on top of the pressed juice is scooped off thus concentrating what is left. The best ice wines come from Canada, Germany and Austria and offer very pure varietal characteristics.

## SPARKLING WINEMAKING METHODS

Simple sparkling wine can be made with low-quality wine, a good dose of sugar, and a good shot of $CO_2$ bubbles in the fashion of cola. The bubbles will be large and rough, as they are in a soft drink. When you buy this sort of wine, a large part of what you pay for is probably tax and very little for the product as the customs tax on sparkling is usually higher (sometimes double) than still wine.

On the other hand, when you buy a PDO champagne or cava, you are guaranteed that it has been made using *méthode traditionelle* via a second fermentation in the bottle, in the manner that Dom Pérignon apparently discovered by chance. It is a controlled second fermentation, with the carbon dioxide produced kept trapped inside the bottle where this second fermentation takes place. The result is smaller, finer bubbles and usually a delicious biscuity touch from the 'autolysis' (self-digestion) of the lees (the leftover dead yeast cells). It is mandatory to state the level of sugar on sparkling wines, while it is optional (but regulated) for other wines. The sugar content of the sparkling wine must be noted usually with the terms 'brut nature', 'zero dosage', 'extra brut' or 'brut' for dry sparkling wine, and with 'demi-sec' for semi-sweet and 'doux' for sweet.

## CHAMPAGNE VERSUS PROSECCO: THE DIFFERENCES

Champagne is from France and Prosecco is from Italy.

Champagne is made with Chardonnay, Pinot Noir and Pinot Meunier grapes. Prosecco is made with the Glera grape.

Champagne has to be made by the more expensive bottle-fermentation method, whereas Prosecco can be made by the less expensive tank method (the second fermentation takes place in a tank then it is bottled).

The Prosecco will be fizzier and lighter, with more fruit and flower aromas. With champagne the bubbles will be finer, sharper and more persistent, and it should have a toasty or biscuity note from its long ageing on the lees in the bottle.

........................................................

## CONCLUSION

Winemaking can make or break good grapes. There are many technologies, additives and techniques available to technologically inclined winemakers that can create wines that are palatable in large volume. However, to create truly great wine takes *terroir*, intention, investment and passion – there are no shortcuts.

........................................................

## CHAPTER 5

# UNDERSTANDING WINE LABELS AND BOTTLES

> 'IT IS BETTER TO HIDE IGNORANCE,
> BUT IT IS HARD TO DO THIS
> WHEN WE RELAX OVER WINE.'
>
> HERACLITUS

. . . . . . . . . . . . . . . . . . . . . . . . . . . . . . . . . . . . . . . . . . . . . . .

Do you feel like Heraclitus? Scared to show your ignorance – especially about wine? Even the most expert experts can be confused in the super complicated world of wine so don't be afraid – ask the waiter or wine shop what the name or the label means if you don't know. For a new wine lover a wine label can be daunting, with loads of tiny print and often foreign words. Labelling of wine is a minefield and, despite EU efforts to make it simpler and to unify wine categories across Europe, each country can still use their own terms in most cases. Globally a wine label generally has to display certain information, including the alcohol level and the contents. Then there are many optional elements that are regulated and usually included, such as the vintage. Other elements that would be useful to you as the wine lover may not be included for reasons of space or concerns about complexity.

# THE REQUIRED LEGISLATED INFORMATION IN MOST COUNTRIES AND WHAT IT TELLS YOU

## The name of the (regulatory) wine category (wine, sparkling wine, fortified wine)

This is more useful if it includes whether it is dry, off-dry, semi-sweet, etc., but this is not required except for champagne.

## The alcoholic strength by volume (shown as a percentage, e.g. 12.5% vol.)

This helps you to know your units of alcohol but also gives an idea of the heaviness of the wine. Usually a lower-alcohol wine will be lighter in style and a higher-alcohol wine will be heavier.

## The provenance (e.g. wine from the European Union, Product of France, Italy, Chile, etc.)

This can help you to understand the style, especially if there are more details about where the wine is from as this can give you an idea of the climate.

## The nominal volume

The standard bottle is 750 ml or 75 cl.

## The bottler's details

The name of the bottler (the natural/legal person who bottles the wine), the bottling headquarters' address (the name of the place and of the EU Member State), followed by the words 'bottler' or 'bottled by'.

## In France, the following terms are common:

*mis en bouteille au château*: estate/château-bottled
*mis en bouteille au domaine*: estate-bottled

## The lot number

The batch number or equivalent, for traceability. Some *appellations* require numbered bottles.

## Health warnings

Alcoholic beverages often require a health warning.

In France the disclaimer that translates as 'The consumption of alcoholic beverages during pregnancy, even in small amounts, can have severe health consequences for a child', or a pictogram to this effect, must be on the bottle.

## A SPLASH OF MILK OR SOME EGG WHITE WITH YOUR WINE?

A new requirement in the EU is the notification of allergens. For wine, the allergen sulphur dioxide must be indicated by 'contains sulphites'.

From 2012, wines that include milk-based products and/or egg-based products (sometimes used for filtration or fining) must mention milk and/or egg if residues of these products are detectable in analysis.

## VINTAGE

Vintage is the year the grapes were picked. To mention 'vintage' on a wine label, at least 85 per cent of the grapes must have been harvested in the year that is quoted as the vintage. In Australia they also call the moment of harvest 'vintage', so for them harvest time is called 'vintage' as well as the year the wine is bottled. In the northern hemisphere harvest is around September and in the southern hemisphere it is around March.

## A VINTAGE YEAR

We also talk of a 'vintage year', meaning a year that was great for wine in a particular region. Excellent old vintages for red Bordeaux include 1945, 1959 and 1961. In more recent times, 2000, 2005, 2009 and 2010 have been hailed as great vintages.

Each vintage is the bottled story of the wine's year of birth. Once you follow the vintages you will taste the differences in different years. Some are more round and accessible; others more angular in youth but beautiful and elegant when a little older.

Some wine writers advise you to only take, for example, the 2005 bottles from one *appellation* or the 2002 bottles from another, or they advise you to only drink young wines to avoid wines that are past their prime. This ruins your fun. Each vintage is a different character with its own unique charm to be discovered. They evolve. With modern winegrowing and winemaking it is rare to find a 'bad vintage', just different vintages and some that will age better than others.

Because some vintages and some styles of wine will age better than others, it is important to know a little about the longevity of a vintage if you are planning to cellar it for the long term.

## SHOULD YOU AGE THE WINE OR NOT?

While most inexpensive, everyday wines are not made to age (so take care about what you lovingly store in your cellar), wines made traditionally can age beautifully, even wines with no sulphites and white wines. You can experiment for yourself with the 'fridge bottle test' below.

### THE FRIDGE BOTTLE TEST

This test offers a very simple way to assess the ageing potential of a wine.

Drink a little less than half the bottle of wine you want to test, make notes about your thoughts, then recork the rest and put it into the fridge. Take a small sample (just enough to taste, aiming to leave close to half of the bottle behind) each day and taste the wine. (If it is red, let it come to room temperature first.) Recork the bottle and replace it in the fridge. If the wine gets better over the days following opening, it has still got many years of life and improvement ahead of it. If it improves the next day then falls apart on the third day, then it has a short life ahead; perhaps a year or two. Usually we say that for every day that a wine improves it has a year or two of ageing potential. If it is not good the day after opening then drink up ASAP as it is unlikely to improve with more ageing.

## GRAPE VARIETY

Similar to vintage labelling, in the EU the name of a single grape variety may be listed alone on the label if the product is made with at least 85 per cent of that variety. In the case of two or more varieties being used, if mention is made of the varieties then all the varieties used must be listed. The variety list should be in descending order from largest component to smallest.

When you have an *appellation* like Châteauneuf-du-Pape where the blend can include up to 13 different varietals, that's a lot of label space.

### LABELLING CAVEATS

Despite all these rules and regulations, recently I bought an Italian Pinot Grigio that was marked Pinot Grigio in dark text with Garganega in very light text above it. I didn't even see the Garganega on the label and the Pinot Grigio (called Pinot Gris in France) was just a small part of the largely Garganega blend – misleading labelling, following the letter of the law but not the spirit.

In some countries, like the USA, the single varietal rule is 75 per cent, so you could have a bottle with 76 per cent Cabernet Sauvignon sold as pure Cabernet Sauvignon.

## WOODCHIPS, BARRELS AND CASKS

Wines marketed in the European Union may bear indications referring to production methods. For example, the words 'barrel' or 'barrel-aged', or 'cask' or 'cask-aged', followed by the name of the wood of the barrel, can be used when the wine has been aged in a wood container and has never been in contact with woodchips. To qualify for this, a wine produced in France, for example, must have been fermented, matured or aged in wooden containers and half of its volume at least must have been in such containers for a minimum period of six months.

### THAT WINE FOR A FIVER COULD NOT HAVE BEEN AGED IN A NEW BARREL

A Bordeaux-style barrel of 225 litres (300 bottles) made from French oak will cost on average €900 including taxes. This means that when ageing wine in new barrels the base cost of the container alone will add about €3 per bottle – and there is an increased labour cost in barrel-ageing too.

## THE 'FARM' IN FRANCE

In France, references to the farm where the wine is produced using the terms château, *domaine*, *clos*, *mas*, etc., are reserved for wines which meet the geographic indication (PDO) plus two other conditions:

1. **THE WINE** must be produced exclusively from grapes harvested in vineyards of the farming entity.

2. **THE WINEMAKING PROCESS** must be fully carried out within the farming entity.

To qualify for the words 'château', '*clos*' or '*cru*', the wines must meet the criteria above *and* have a designation of origin (PDO).

## GERMAN QUALITY

In Germany the regulatory quality-labelling system, *Qualitätswein mit Prädikat*, goes from *Kabinett* (light wines made from the least ripe grapes) to *Trockenbeerenauslese* (TBA) (intense, noble wines made from the most ripe grapes). The word *trocken* here means the grapes have dried and started to shrivel, so the wine is very sweet, rather than the word 'trocken' on its own on a German label, which would refer to 'dry', i.e. not sweet.

### THE FRAUD SQUAD

The labelling of French wine is strictly controlled. Comprehensive rules are diligently enforced by a dedicated 'fraud squad'. There is no leeway for loose marketing statements and contravention means a hefty fine and/or jail. This means that what French labels claim is usually correct.

## SOME TERMS REGULARLY USED BUT NOT FORMALLY DEFINED OR REGULATED

- **Réserve/Grand Réserve** (but Reserva and Gran Reserva is regulated for Rioja and Riserva for some DOCs in Italy like Chianti: indicating higher levels of quality and ageing than the standard product).

- **Grand Vin**: Directly translated this means 'great wine' and it is used on the top wine made by a winegrower but it is a totally unregulated term that anyone can use for any wine.

- **Winemaker's selection**: No regulated meaning.

- **Gold medal standard**: No accepted/official meaning (other than for marketing purposes).

- **Old vines**: The vines are usually taken to be older than 40 years but since this is not regulated it depends on the grower.

### TUTANKHAMUN'S WINE LABELS

Several jars of wine were found in the tomb of Tutankhamun, the famous Egyptian king who died at a very young age in c.1327 BC. The jars, discovered in 1922, were labelled with the wine's name, the vintage, the source and even the winegrower. The wine had dried out by the time it was discovered – not surprising given that well over 3,000 years had passed. Nevertheless, a team of Spanish scientists determined that the jars had contained red wine because of remnants specific to red wine.

## HOW ARE WINE PRICES DETERMINED?

The price of a wine bottle usually reflects, at least partly, the costs that went into producing it. Some producers can demand a premium well beyond the total costs that went into the wine, though, because of their reputation, quality, marketing or a perfect score from a powerful wine critic.

So what are some of the costs?

- **The land**: the purchase cost in the Champagne region is around €1,000,000 per hectare, whereas in the Languedoc region it is around €12,000 per hectare.

- **The method of farming**: low yield and/or more work carried out by hand equals higher cost. Vineyards are in any event very labour-intensive, with one of the highest 'manhours per hectare' rates of all farming.

- **The method of winemaking**: small-lot individual wines and/or barrel-ageing equals higher cost.

- **The winery and farming equipment**: a top-quality peristaltic wine pump used by high-end wineries can cost €10,000, while an everyday rotor pump used by most wineries can cost less than €1,000.

- **The bottling and packaging**: a cork can range from a couple of cents to more than a euro.

- **The marketing and selling of the wine**.

## WHY DO SOME BOTTLES COST SO MUCH?

The most expensive wines have gained, and can maintain, their status with historical prestige, excellent ratings by powerful critics and marketing. It is also about demand and supply. A wine that has a very high reputation but relatively low production has this simple economic principle on its side.

## THE MOST EXPENSIVE WINE BOTTLE EVER

An imperial bottle (the equivalent of eight standard bottles) of 1947 Cheval Blanc, a St-Emilion *Grand Cru Classé* A, was sold at auction for £192,000 in November 2010 to a private collector. In 2013, a case of 12 bottles of 1978 Romanée-Conti went for £295,838, beating the previous record based on a standard bottle-for-bottle calculation. That's nearly £5,000 per 150 ml glass!

## WHAT DOES THE BOTTLE SHAPE SAY ABOUT THE WINE?

Sometimes the bottle shape is legislated, like the tall, slim and elegant upside-down tulip shape in Alsace, which is often used for Alsatian-style wines, even for a Riesling from as far away as Clare Valley in Australia. For Burgundy, the Loire and the Rhône valley, and wines made in these styles, it is usually the sloped bottle. For wines in the Bordeaux region and Bordeaux-style wines, it is the straight-sided and tall-shouldered bottle; this is not enforced but is generally followed.

THE ALSACE BOTTLE

THE B
BO

UNDY
LE

THE BORDEAUX
BOTTLE

## PLANNING A PARTY? CONSIDER A LARGE FORMAT BOTTLE

A large bottle provides better ageing (because the ageing will be slower) than a small bottle, so choose a magnum or an even bigger bottle if you can afford it. If you are buying ahead for a future party, a magnum or double magnum can be great. Once you go over the imperial, you will struggle to pour the wine.

## BOTTLE SIZES

**0.375 litre demi**
(a half bottle. 'Demi' means 'half' in French)

**0.5 litre jennie**
(a 500-ml bottle, often used for sweet wines)

**0.750 litre**
(the standard bottle size)

**1.5 litre magnum**

**3.0 litre jeroboam**
(aka double magnum)

**6.0 litre imperial**

**9.0 litre salmanazar**
(named after an Assyrian king)

**12.0 litre balthazar**
(named after a king of Babylon)

**15.0 litre nebuchadnezzar**
(named after another king of Babylon)

**18.0 litre melchior**
(named after one of the Three Wise Men).
That's 24 standard bottles in one bottle!
Better order a special machine to pour this
one... Yes, you can!

# FRENCH WINE TERMS AND THEIR ENGLISH MEANINGS

| French term | English meaning |
| --- | --- |
| *blanc sec* | dry white |
| *brut* | dry sparkling wine |
| *cave* | cellar |
| *cépage* | grape variety |
| *chai* (pronounced 'shai') | winery |
| *château* | a wine estate which may or may not have a castle or manor house on it |
| *clos* | a walled vineyard (sometimes the wall is gone but the vineyard still bears the name) |
| *côte* | hillside |
| *coteaux* | hillsides |
| *cru* | 'growth', generally indicates a specific high-quality vineyard, district or village |
| *cru classé* | classified vineyard (in Bordeaux particularly) |
| *cuve* | vat or tank |
| *cuvée* | blend or lot |
| *demi-sec* | medium dry |
| *domaine* | estate |

| French term | English meaning |
|---|---|
| *doux* | sweet |
| *eau-de-vie* | spirit |
| *fût de chêne* | oak barrel (aged in) |
| *grand cru* | 'great growth', a legislated term in France meaning a vineyard designated as offering great potential in an official ranking |
| *grand cru classé* | 'great classified growth', a legislated term in France meaning a vineyard classed as 'great' in an official ranking |
| *grand vin de* | marketing term meaning 'great wine of' with no legal significance |
| *liquoreux* | a full sweet wine (e.g. Saussignac or Sauternes) |
| *marc* | pomace – the residue of skins after pressing |
| *mas* | term for a farm or farmhouse often used in Provence and Languedoc |
| *mis en bouteille* | bottled |
| *mis en bouteille au château* | estate-bottled |
| *négociant* | a merchant who buys wine to mature or bottle/resell |
| *propriétaire* | owner |
| *raisin* | grape |
| *récoltant* | harvester of grapes |

| French term | English meaning |
|---|---|
| *récolte* | harvest/vintage |
| *rouge* | red |
| *sec* | dry |
| *supérieur (Bordeaux)* | indicates an extra 0.5% to 1% vol. alcohol |
| *vendange* | vintage/harvest |
| *vignoble* | vineyard |
| *vigne* | vine |

## CONCLUSION

Knowing how to read different labels makes your wine-purchasing easier. The label can tell you much about a wine, but perhaps not as much as you would like to know. You may find more information about the wine on the winegrower's website, including such details as the barrel-ageing, whether it did the 'malo' or not, the level of acidity and the sweetness level. Learning to read and understand labels will help you choose wine wisely, and help immeasurably when choosing the right wine to go with your food at home and in a restaurant.

# CHAPTER 6

# PAIRING FOOD AND WINE

'I ENJOY COOKING WITH WINE; SOMETIMES
I EVEN PUT IT IN THE FOOD.'

ATTRIBUTED TO JULIA CHILD

. . . . . . . . . . . . . . . . . . . . . . . . . . . . . . . . . . . . . . . . . . . . . . . . . . . .

Have you ever wondered why some classic matches
– like botrytis dessert wine with Roquefort cheese,
or a Bordeaux blend with a rare fillet steak – work
so perfectly? Wine and food perfectly paired bring a
higher level of enjoyment. France is a specialist at this
aspect of wine: courses are mapped out with specific
wines and often the meal is planned around the wines.
In this chapter we explore the guiding principles of

pairing. With these you can assess food and wine for yourself, see why classics work and create new matches to suit your taste.

## A WIDE FIELD OF PAIRING

There is a very wide set of options in the world of pairing, given all the different dishes and all the different wines available today. Given the enormity of options, a list of 'this with that' is of limited use.

## UNDERSTAND WHAT YOU LIKE

What you like is the most important thing. If you only like dry wine then don't drink sweet wine, even when you have Roquefort; you can find an alternative that works for you. If you like red wine then don't drink white even when you eat white fish; there are light, low-tannin reds that could work, like a Beaujolais.

In the grand scheme of pairing, there are principles and there are certain pairings that are 'no-nos', but for each dish there are many wine options. We are all different and personal preferences do matter, plus there is a large middle ground of most wines being relatively palatable for most people with most foods. However, it really pays to seek out the magical pairings because when you find them it is pure heaven, with both the food and the wine raised to a higher level.

## FLAVOUR VERSUS TASTE AND SMELL

Flavour is a combination of taste and smell. What we think is taste is often smell, as our tongues only perceive four main elements: sweet, salt, bitter and acid. Relatively recently, a fifth taste called umami was identified in Japan and is broadly defined as harmonious (imagine the ultimate ripe tomato, a perfect harmony of sweet and savoury, and you have the idea).

### DEVELOP YOUR SENSE OF AROMA BY DISCONNECTING YOUR NOSE FROM YOUR EYES

Our sense of smell developed long before our language ability, so it is a very ancient skill. We are accustomed to seeing what we smell so it is often difficult to recognise the aroma without seeing the thing that would produce that aroma. One of the ways I suggest for learning to pick out wine aromas is to train your brain to smell without seeing. Close your eyes and take in the aromas of fruits and spices (e.g. when cooking in the kitchen or eating breakfast). Even away from the kitchen, for example in the office, smell the pencil shavings at your desk (sometimes we pick up the aroma of pencil shavings on Merlot red wines). Doing this can help develop your capability to define the aromas of a wine, a useful tool in wine and food pairing. Women are seen as generally better tasters than men, perhaps harking back to their task of 'gatherer', when knowledge of what you were picking for your family and avoidance of poison meant life or death.

# THE COMPONENTS OF WINE

To assess the food pairing potential of a wine, you need an idea of the level of each of the five main components of a wine: alcohol, acids, tannins, sugar and aromas. These elements will help you think about which food they can pair with. Along the same lines of the tasting chapter, we'll take each of these in turn.

## 1. ALCOHOL

Alcohol creates a sensation of sweetness and masks aggressive acids and tannins. The higher the alcohol, the weightier the wine.

**How to sense alcohol**

Alcohol produces a warmth – or burning in the case of very high-content alcohol – on the back of the throat. You can look at the level of alcohol on the bottle, but you can also develop an ability to assess it from taste and sensation.

## 2. ACIDITY

Acidity provides verve and a backbone to a wine, as well as a sensation of freshness and crispness. The two primary acids in wine are tartaric acid and malic acid. In most red wines and some white wines, the 'green apple' malic acid is converted to a softer, more buttery lactic acid by malo (malolactic fermentation) – this is effectively a deacidification, so before malo it is more acidic and after less so. Whether a wine has done its malo has an impact on its overall character and what it matches with. Acidity decreases the weight and richness of a wine and provides a lift.

A wine's acidity decreases with time and a good level of acidity helps a wine to age gracefully and retain its youth. Acidity is naturally higher in organic and biodynamic wines because chemical fertilisers make a grape vine lower its acidity. This acidity is part of the overall harmony of a wine and also allows natural winegrowers to use lower levels of sulphur dioxide, the preservative used in wine, since the natural acid acts as a preservative.

### How to sense acidity

When you taste a wine, you will find the level of acidity with the sensors in the back of your cheeks and sides of the back half of your tongue. Acidic wines make your mouth water.

## 3. TANNINS

Tannins come from the grape skins and provide structure and some of the colour and flavour to red wine. Tannins are antioxidants and protect a wine, thus increasing its ageing potential, but they can also mask flavour if they are at a high level. As a wine ages, the tannins soften. Along with tannins from the skins, we can also find oak tannin from barrel-ageing.

### ANCIENT WINEMAKING, GEORGIAN STYLE

Most white wine grapes are pressed and the skins removed quickly, but some ancient methods of white winemaking include the skins and create very interesting and different wines, like the traditional-method white wines of Georgia.

### How to sense tannin

A sense of dryness on your gums and roughness in your mouth indicates tannin. Tannins bind with and remove salivary proteins that lubricate the mouth, thus creating the sensation of dryness. They do the same to proteins in food, thereby helping digestion and hence the classic match of a rare steak with a high-tannin Pauillac red wine from Bordeaux (which consists of barrel-aged Cabernet Sauvignon and Merlot).

The more cooked the steak, the less tannin it supports. A well-cooked steak would be best matched with a fruitier, less tannic, red wine. Take the same piece of meat and cook it half very rare and half very well done, then compare the two with a tannic young red wine (e.g. Pauillac) and perhaps a low-tannin Grenache blend (e.g. a light Côtes-du-Rhône) to see this for yourself. It is the ability of tannin to bind with and to remove protein that produces the drying-out sensation on your gums and also releases more flavour from your rare steak.

## TANNINS FOR TANNING HIDE

An easy way to remember the effect of this aspect of wine is that we use the tannin from trees to tan hides to turn them into leather.

**Beware of pairing tannic wines with fish or umami foods**

Umami foods typically do not pair with tannic wines as the tannins are accentuated, so save the mushroom dish or slow-cooked tomato stew for a lower tannin wine.

Tannins in combination with oily fish, like mackerel, create an unpleasant metallic taste.

## 4. SUGAR OR SWEETNESS

The fourth component is residual sugar: sugar that has not been converted to alcohol at the end of the fermentation process. This can be natural grape sugar expressly kept from fermenting, concentrated grape juice added at the end of the fermentation, or even (horror) added cane or beet sugar. Sugar increases the body of the wine and can alleviate high tannin and acid.

**How to sense sweetness**

You taste sweetness on your tongue and sweetness also tends to make you thirsty.

## 5. FLAVOURS AND AROMAS

Youthful wines often display floral and fruity aromas, while older wines offer 'developed' aromas associated with ageing, like mushrooms, truffles, leather, nuts, chocolate or cigar box. Red wines generally have red or dark fruit aromas, while white wines have lighter-colour fruit aromas, like citrus, stone fruits, tropical fruits, apple or pear. Varietals (grape types) have typical aromas that help us identify them in blind tastings: for example, blackberry and plum in Merlot. The aromas and other elements give us the 'character' of the wine. For example, a young Cabernet Sauvignon is full-bodied, tannic and acidic with aromas of blackcurrant and perhaps cedar. Once you can identify aromas, you can use them for your pairing choices. For instance, a young Sauvignon Blanc can offer notes of grapefruit zest; if you put a shaving of grapefruit zest on the salad you plan to serve with the Sauvignon this can turn it from interesting to 'wow'.

## How to sense flavours and aromas

We smell the aromas and specific flavours rather than taste them. We taste the basic characters of sweet, salt, bitter and acid but then the nuances like peach are actually aromas picked up through the back of our nose – known as the 'retro-olfactory' sense of smell. Picking them up requires training your nose to know the aroma without your eyes needing to see it.

## Oak's effect

Ageing in oak changes the profile of a wine, making it richer, more full-bodied, and bringing additional aromas like vanilla or spice. This impacts potential food matches. For example, an unoaked Chablis would be perfect with simple seafood, while an oaked Chardonnay would be better with seafood in creamy sauce.

## How to sense oak

You can pick up aromas of barrel-ageing including vanilla, toasty characters and sweet spices. These aromas depend on where the oak is from and how much 'toasting' the barrel had on the inside. Light toast can give coconut and some sweet spice; heavy toast can give grilled coffee or cocoa beans. The wood is heated to bend it into the shape of the barrel and extra time and/or extra heat at this moment produces a 'toasting' effect on the wood that then offers these different aromas to the wine that is stored in the barrel. There are a million variations of barrel maker, forest and toast.

## AMERICAN OAK VERSUS FRENCH OAK

American oak is generally faster growing and wider grain, part of the reason its barrels are usually about half the price of French oak. It is also why the aromas are more forward and upfront, often marked 'coconut', while the French oak aromas are more discreet and offer classic vanilla and spice aromas.

# THE PRINCIPLES OF WINE AND FOOD PAIRING

Matching up the characteristics of the food and the wine using the three key elements of weight/richness, acidity and flavour will help you find great pairing combinations for the foods you like to eat. The sauce and cooking method are as important as whether the food is vegetable, meat or fish.

## 1. MATCH UP THE WEIGHT OR RICHNESS OF THE FOOD WITH THE WEIGHT AND BODY OF THE WINE

The first thing to consider is the weight of the primary ingredients of the food and the sauce, then match these with the body of the wine.

## The primary elements that affect the weight:

- The sauce: think of a squeeze of lemon and compare with a rich, creamy sauce.

- The temperature: cold is lighter than hot.

- The type of cooking: raw-salmon sushi is lighter than fried salmon.

- The fat content: low-fat items or lean cuts are lighter than high-fat ones.

Typically, a weighty wine must be matched with a weighty food, but overly rich with overly rich may be too much, so if you serve a rich food with a rich wine find one that also has high acid and/or tannin. This will help to decrease the sensation of richness in a wine and lift the experience. For example, a rich lamb dish works well with a Bordeaux-blend wine.

## WEIGHT PAIRING EXAMPLES

- Pan-fried white fish with a squeeze of lemon: a bright, acidic white wine, like Muscadet or Sauvignon Blanc.

- Rare steak with salad: this medium-weight dish would be good with a tannic and acidic red, like a Cabernet Sauvignon.

- Duck breast with sweet spices: this medium- to heavyweight dish would be magic with a spicy, barrel-aged Merlot. Duck and Merlot are made for each other and the barrel-ageing brings the hint of spice.

- Vegan lemon and pea risotto: this bright, light dish is another great match with a Sauvignon Blanc. The acidity and citrus fruit of Sauvignon Blanc are perfect with lemon.

**Match up the texture of the food and the texture of the wine**

We can also consider the texture of the food and the wine. Chewy meats and foods high in protein, like rare beef, are ideal with tannic wines as the tannins help to break down the meat and the meat helps to soften the tannins. Creamy foods match with creamy wines, e.g. seafood in a creamy sauce with a barrel-aged Sémillon.

The character and culture of a food can generate a good wine match, like Alsatian choucroute (sauerkraut) with a Pinot Gris from Alsace.

### HOT SOUP AND COLD WINE? A DIFFICULT PAIRING

Hot soup and cold wine conflict, making this a difficult pairing. Identifying the main components of the soup and matching it using the principles is still a good way forward, for example a creamy seafood chowder could be paired with a barrel-aged white wine.

## 2. ACIDITY

Acidity in wine is key for pairing with food. Usually wines that work with food need a good dose of it. A soft, easy-drinking, aperitif wine will not benefit a meal. Imagine 'the drop of lemon juice test': if the food improves with a drop of lemon then you need a high-acid wine. Think of a simple, pan-fried white fish: perfect with an acidic Muscadet. Or a zesty, tomato-based pasta dish: great with a Chianti made of Sangiovese that has a good level of acid.

## REGIONAL FOODS WITH REGIONAL WINES

It is interesting that the traditional foods of a region are the ones that pair well with the local wines. Think of the western seaboard of the Loire valley in France, where Muscadet is. The cuisine is all about seafood: white fish, mussels, oysters – all the things that match perfectly with Muscadet wine. Then think of the food the Tuscans eat: tomato-based dishes that are rich with olive oil and need a wine with good acidity to match up to the acidity of the tomatoes and to cut through the olive oil – bring on the Chianti.

The acidity of the wine is not only dependent on the grape type but also on the climate and the decision of when to harvest. Cooler climates mean more acidity, and hotter climates mean less. Organic wines contain more natural acidity than chemically farmed wines. Always keep the acidity of the wine at least as high as the food or the wine will appear flat. In addition, oily foods or heavily fried foods need wines with good acidity to cut through their richness.

## EXAMPLES OF TYPICALLY HIGH-ACID VARIETALS AND THEIR *APPELLATIONS*

- White: Melon de Bourgogne (Muscadet), Riesling (Alsace), cool-climate Chardonnay (Champagne, unoaked Chablis), Sauvignon Blanc (Sancerre).

- Red: Cabernet Sauvignon (Bordeaux blends), Gamay (Beaujolais), Nebbiolo (Barolo), Sangiovese (Chianti).

## EXAMPLES OF TYPICALLY LOW-ACID VARIETALS AND THEIR *APPELLATIONS*

- White: Viognier (Rhône white), hot-climate Chardonnay (Paso Robles).

- Red: Zinfandel (Napa Valley), hot-climate Tempranillo (Valdepeñas).

## 3. FLAVOURS: COMPLEMENT OR CONTRAST?

Being able to define the flavours and aromas of a wine and their intensity can help to match the wine with the right food. Once we know the aromas and flavours, we can match the intensity, reflect the flavours or even add elements to the meal to complement them. For example, if you pick up a hint of clove in the wine, put a clove into the reduction sauce you are making.

### Intensity: find the balance

A light, delicate food like poached white fish would not match well with an intense, aromatic grape like Gewürztraminer; it would match with a light, bright Muscadet. The Gewürztraminer would go better with an intense, spicy Thai chicken. Intense food flavours like saltiness, sweetness, spiciness and smokiness need wines that can match their intensity or the wine will be crushed.

### Reflecting flavours

Reflecting the flavours in the food with those in the wine can also work well. For example, Zinfandel's smokiness means that it pairs well with smoked or BBQ food.

---

**Important flavour tips**

- If you are using wine in cooking, serve exactly the same wine at the table. This guarantees reflecting flavours.

- If you are serving a wine that has signature flavours of plum and blackberry, like a Merlot, serving a sauce that contains plums or blackberry (for example, duck breast with a blackberry reduction sauce) will be superb.

- If there is a side dish with the main then connecting the wine with the side dish can also work. For example, white fish with lemon sauce and fresh garden peas with an older Sauvignon Blanc (as Sauvignon Blanc ages, the asparagus tones change to green pea tones).

- Always consider all the elements of the food experience, including sauce and sides.

---

## Complementing flavours

Another useful technique is complementing the flavours in the food. If a food is regularly complemented by a certain accompaniment, then choose a wine containing that element. For example, choose a wine with elements of cranberry, like a dry rosé made from Cabernet Sauvignon, to go with turkey and cranberry sauce.

## Umami, the fifth taste

'Umami', the fifth taste, was defined in Japan. It means harmonious, savoury, delicious and is like the taste of MSG (monosodium glutamate).

Umami can be increased in meat by stewing, curing, ageing or smoking, and in vegetables by processing or drying. Sundried tomatoes have more than fresh tomatoes. Foods rich in umami include seaweed, cheese, very ripe tomatoes, mushrooms and mackerel.

Tannins can clash with umami, so young tannic red wines are not a great match; old wines where the tannins have softened or red wines with good acidity but lower tannin are better.

## Sweet with sweet

Like acidity, the sweetness of the wine must be at least as high as the sweetness of the food. If the food is sweeter than the wine then the wine can appear out of balance and the acidity will be accentuated. For sweet and spicy foods, like sweet and sour pork, it is best to go for a lower-alcohol, semi-sweet wine like some of those from Alsace or Germany.

## Saltiness accentuates tannin and can enhance sweetness

In general, saltiness accentuates tannins so salty foods go best with white wines, rosés or reds with very low tannins like Beaujolais. Salty foods can be enhanced by sweetness, such as Roquefort cheese by Saussignac dessert wine. The saltiness of oysters would be best with a crisp, dry white based on the weight and acidity. Typically, salty should be matched with wines with a good level of acidity: salt creates a sense of acidity, which makes low-acid wines appear flat and out of balance, so acidic white wines are best.

## Smoked foods with intense wines

Smoked foods need relatively intense wines to match up to this powerful element. Smoked salmon is classically matched with brut champagne or an oaked white wine, while smoky BBQ red meats would be ideal with a smoky Zinfandel or Shiraz. Smoke also goes with oak.

## Spicy foods with Alsace-style wines

Lightly spiced foods can be matched with wines such as those from Alsace or Germany, including light, medium-sweet styles from Gewürztraminer, a semi-sweet Chenin Blanc from Vouvray in the Loire or a moelleux (sweet wine) from Bergerac. For extremely hot, spiced foods, forget the wine and go for beer or water.

### SALAD AND WINE: ANOTHER DIFFICULT PAIRING

Look at all the components of your salad and make your assessment based on the principles of weight, acidity and flavour. Vinegar is often used in salad dressing and typically does not match well with wine. A handy trick is to substitute the vinegar in the dressing with the wine you will serve with the salad. It needs to be acidic – a soft wine won't work.

## The cheese plate: tricky choices

Red wine with cheese? Many of us have this idea, but if you try it for yourself you will find that white wines usually match best with soft cheese and stronger flavours. Fresh goat's cheese with dry Sauvignon Blanc is a classic, as is dessert wine with Roquefort. Red wines can pair with hard cheese and some milder flavour soft cheese. It is also a matter of personal taste: if you like red with your cheese, stick to red.

## PAIRING QUIZ

What wine would you choose to match with the following foods? Choose a, b or c.

1. Roast lamb:
   a. brut champagne
   b. dry full-bodied rosé
   c. red Bordeaux

2. Chicken korma:
   a. Viognier
   b. red Côtes-du-Rhône
   c. dry Sauvignon Blanc

3. Mussels in white wine:
   a. Beaujolais nouveau
   b. Bordeaux rosé
   c. Muscadet dry white

4. Rare steak:
   a. aged red Burgundy
   b. young red Bordeaux
   c. German Riesling

5. Chicken & mushroom pie:
   a. Chardonnay
   b. Shiraz/Syrah
   c. dessert wine

6. Vegan lemon pea risotto:
   a. Gewürztraminer
   b. Sauvignon Blanc
   c. Grenache red

## CONCLUSION

Pairing food and wine is fun. When you find a great combination it can bring an extra layer of appreciation to the occasion. There are some pairings that are truly exceptional, others that are OK and some that are awful. *Bonne dégustation!* Happy tasting! Enjoying wine and food is part of appreciating wine in moderation and enjoying it as part of a healthy diet.

## CHAPTER 7

# WINE AND
# YOUR HEALTH

'I HAVE ENJOYED GREAT HEALTH
AT A GREAT AGE BECAUSE EVERY
DAY SINCE I CAN REMEMBER I HAVE
CONSUMED A BOTTLE OF WINE, EXCEPT
WHEN I HAVE NOT FELT WELL. THEN
I HAVE CONSUMED TWO BOTTLES.'

BISHOP OF SEVILLE

..........................................................

Wine is a health drink; it is packed with vitamins and minerals. There have been many studies about the health benefits of a glass of red wine in the evening with your dinner. But the idea that a glass of wine can be beneficial must be accompanied by an understanding that alcohol is a poison and that alcoholism is a disease. Not only that, but alcohol is one of the biggest causes of death in road accidents. So wine is something to enjoy and respect while remaining well aware of the risks it presents if not treated responsibly.

## THE FRENCH PARADOX
## AND ANTIOXIDANTS

The 'French Paradox' was a phrase coined for the strange fact that the French eat a lot of fat in the form of butter, cheese and cream (and drink a lot of wine) but have fewer heart attacks than nations that eat less fat (and drink less wine).

A glass of red wine with your dinner offers enjoyment, relaxation and also a dose of resveratrol, a polyphenol plant compound that is an antioxidant thought to help combat the effects of ageing and protect against heart disease.

## KNOW THE LIMITS

Alcohol is legally restricted in most countries. There are age limits to buying drink, blood alcohol limits for driving, restrictions covering the marketing of alcohol and generally accepted responsible drinking guidelines.

## IT'S OFFICIAL: GALS CAN'T DRINK BLOKES UNDER THE TABLE

Even if a man and a woman are the same size and weight, alcohol disperses in body water and, pound for pound, women have less water in their bodies than men do, so a woman can drink less alcohol than a man the same size.

## Blood alcohol concentration and driving under the influence

Most countries have set limits for blood alcohol concentration when driving or operating machinery. For many of us, this is equivalent to a small glass of wine. In some places like Russia, the limit is zero: that way there is no temptation. To avoid a fine or worse, a tragedy, having a designated driver or finding alternative transport is the way to go.

## Responsible drinking guidelines

The UK's responsible drinking guidelines state:

1.  Maximum 3–4 units (24–32 g) per day and maximum 21 units (168 g) per week for men
2.  Maximum 2–3 units (16–24 g) per day and maximum 14 units (112 g) per week for women
3.  Women who are pregnant, or trying to become pregnant, and who choose to drink, should drink no more than 1–2 units of alcohol per week.

This assumes a unit is 8 g of alcohol.

In addition to these guidelines, try not to exceed four units on any one occasion and try to have one or two alcohol-free days a week.

## WHEN IS A GLASS NOT A GLASS?

One glass of wine is not necessarily equivalent to another. If we take an average glass of wine of 150 ml at 12% alcohol volume, it amounts to 2.25 units, whereas the same glass of wine at 14.5% alcohol volume amounts to 2.72 units. This uses a UK unit of 8 g of pure alcohol (whereas the WHO sets the unit at 10–12 g). In a litre of wine at 12% alcohol volume, there is 120 ml or 120 g of pure alcohol, so about 15 units – converting that to a standard 750 ml bottle, we have about 11.25 units, so if you share a bottle of wine you are well over the recommended amount per day.

A bit like calorie-counting, constant counting can destroy the enjoyment. Keeping to the guiding principle that wine is to be enjoyed and respected is a good place to start.

## THE DANGERS OF DRUNKENNESS

It is well to be aware that too much drink is dangerous even if you are not driving. A person under the influence of drink has an increased risk of injury, a greater risk of having unsafe sex, an increased risk of fights and arguments, plus the risk of alcohol poisoning, coma and brain damage.

## THE DANGERS OF REGULAR OVERCONSUMPTION OF ALCOHOL

When it comes to long-term dependence on alcohol, dangers include cirrhosis of the liver, stomach disorders, increased risk of certain types of cancer, and family- and job-related difficulties.

### DON'T FORGET THE CALORIES...

In this age of obesity, it is important to flag up that alcohol consumption means calorie consumption too. The UK Drinkaware website www.drinkaware. co.uk provides a calorie calculator. A glass of 175 ml (i.e. a quarter of a bottle) of 13% wine is 2.3 units and 159 calories, which is equivalent to half a standard burger and requires about 16 minutes of serious running to work off. If you drink half a bottle it is like eating a whole burger. Like with everything, moderation is key.

## ALCOHOLISM IN HISTORY

Widespread drunkenness and alcoholism were first noted in around 100 BC and they became so common that they (along with some economic reasons) incited the emperor Domitian to pass the first wine laws in AD 92, banning new plantings in Rome and demanding half of the vineyards in the Provinces be uprooted. The laws were largely ignored and officially repealed in AD 280 by Probius.

## TAXES ON WINE

There are customs taxes on wine in most countries as a way to raise funds and to counteract the negative effects of alcohol. I agree with Thomas Jefferson who said:

*'I think it is a great error to consider a heavy tax on wines as a tax on luxury. On the contrary, it is a tax on the health of our citizens.'*

........................................................

## CONCLUSION

Wine can enhance our lives and our health when taken respectfully and in moderation, but it has the potential to be addictive and to destroy health and life if abused. Wine is to be enjoyed responsibly. *Vive le vin!*

........................................................

# CHAPTER 8

# WINE PERSONALITIES, FILMS AND BOOKS

'THE WINE URGES ME ON, THE BEWITCHING WINE, WHICH SETS EVEN A WISE MAN TO SINGING AND TO LAUGHING GENTLY AND ROUSES HIM UP TO DANCE AND BRINGS FORTH WORDS WHICH WERE BETTER UNSPOKEN.'

HOMER'S *ODYSSEY*

The world of wine is a rich tapestry of hearty characters that sing, dance and offer irreverent commentary, from ancient times through to today. There are many great 'wine moments' in modern screen culture, even when the subject matter isn't wine, from James Bond's view on the temperature of champagne in *Goldfinger* to Basil's comment on Bordeaux and Claret in *Fawlty Towers*. In popular culture we find actors dabbling in wine, wine films to enjoy with a glass in hand and wine books to browse.

## WINE DYNASTIES
The world of wine dynasties is packed with intrigue. Each of these families offers a plethora of interesting characters and history that could make a book in itself.

### The Antinoris and Frescobaldis
The Antinoris and the Frescobaldis are important players in Italian wine, and both are Florentine families that made their fortunes in wine and banking. Theirs are very long family histories, going back 26 and 30 generations respectively.

Ludovico, part of the Antinori family, was behind the innovative 'Super Tuscan' Ornellaia, a new form of Tuscan wine made from international varieties, instead of 100 per cent Sangiovese, the traditional grape of the region. This Super Tuscan is geographically next door to Sassicaia, the original Super Tuscan started by Piero, a cousin of the head of the Antinori dynasty, who has his own Super Tuscan estate called Solaia.

Ornellaia vineyard and winery was bought by the Mondavis in 2002 at the same time that they were initiating a partnership with the Frescobaldis, the ancient adversaries of the Antinoris. In 2005, in a weird twist worthy of Shakespeare, the Frescobaldis bought the shares of Ornellaia from Constellation, who had taken over the Robert Mondavi Winery (see the Mondavi entry), and thereby came to own this famous Antinori winery. This is just one story in a family history spanning over 600 years. For more, read Piero Antinori's autobiography *The Hills of Chianti*.

### The Rothschilds
In the late 1700s, the Rothschild family's sons were sent to different corners of the earth to make their fortunes. They achieved this, starting what became a household name in the banking and wine sectors.

In 1853, Nathaniel Rothschild was the first to buy a château, in Médoc in the Bordeaux area: Château Brane-Mouton, which he renamed Mouton Rothschild. Next door to Mouton is Lafite, purchased by James Rothschild in 1868. Both are completely separate family businesses run by different branches of the Rothschild family. Lafite was already a *premier grand cru classé* when it was purchased. Mouton was classified a *deuxième* (second) at the time but became a *premier* through state decree by Jacques Chirac in 1973. It is a famous estate at the head of an empire that now includes the industrial branded wine Mouton Cadet, several estates across the globe and various *grands crus classés*.

## The Torres

The Torres family story started in Penedès, Spain, around 1870. Jaime Torres made his fortune in Cuba in the 1800s and came back to found a winery with his brother, a winegrower in Penedès. They created a large bulk winery that was subsequently destroyed during the Spanish Civil War.

A fourth-generation member of the family, Miguel, rebuilt the winery and started again in 1940. He rebuilt with a view to bottling and labelling his wine rather than creating bulk wine this time. With France under Hitler's control, Miguel took the opportunity to travel to the USA to promote his wines and made his first mark on the American market, a key step in building the brand.

Today Torres is a huge wine brand. Drinks International awarded them the 'World's Most Admired Wine Brand' in 2015. Torres has grown to include vineyards in Chile and California, and is the largest producer of DO (denomination of origin) wines produced under its own label in Spain.

## The Mondavis

The Mondavi wine story is a family history that could be a soap-opera script. Their story was started by Rosa and Césare Mondavi, Italian immigrants who settled in California and bought their first winery in 1943. However, it was their son, Robert Mondavi, who raised the family to dynasty status after breaking away from the core family business after a feud with his brother Peter.

Robert established his own operation, the Robert Mondavi Winery, and his innovative marketing and exceptional energy, passion and drive, along with varietal labelling – a new approach at the time – helped grow his business into a powerhouse of the Napa Valley and beyond. He also created a joint venture with the Rothschilds of Mouton Rothschild called Opus One, an iconic estate in Napa Valley.

Robert built his wine business into a very successful and high-profile entity. Then, to maximise its value, he listed it on the stock exchange in the early 1990s, generating significant wealth for his family but also opening the business to a controversial takeover by Constellation Brands in 2004. The family lost control.

They had also lost their way commercially by going into higher-volume, lower-quality wines and losing their image that had been founded on high-end wine.

The family started again with a premium winery called Continuum that is run by Robert Mondavi's son Tim, daughter Marcia and several of his grandchildren. The best-selling book *The House of Mondavi* gives a great overview of the creation and eventual destruction of Robert Mondavi's empire and offers an entertaining read.

## Gallo

The Gallo family is an American wine family with a history that reads like a thriller. The founding father, Joseph Gallo, died in a 'suicide murder'. Officially, Joseph killed his wife then turned the gun on himself, but some believe it was a Mafia killing. Joseph's sons, Ernest and Julio, started E & J Gallo Winery, now the biggest exporter of Californian wines and also the world's largest family-owned winery. They were canny, creating a product that was like jelly and when mixed with water became wine, a clever innovation for disguising wine during prohibition, and they moved on from there. E & J Gallo Winery is now run by two of Julio's grandchildren, Matt and Gina. Gina is married to Jean-Charles Boisset, part of the wine family that is Burgundy's largest wine producer.

## Primum Familiae Vini

When looking for a list of top wine families, you are almost sure to stumble across a group whose name is a bit of a Latin mouthful, Primum Familiae Vini (PFV). This informal association of top wine families was created in 1993 after two wine moguls, Miguel Torres and Robert Drouhin, were chatting about common challenges as they walked through a vineyard. They realised that the top family-owned vineyards faced similar challenges and could share ideas and best practice – and have fun in the process. They set up a group that includes the world's most prestigious family-owned wineries – a luxurious group of producers who exude prestige and power in the world of wine.

Originally the group included: the Antinoris of Tuscany; the Symington family of English origin (known primarily for their ports); the Drouhin family, originally of Burgundy; Egon Müller, a 200-year-old family estate based in the Mosel in Germany; the Hugels, winegrowers since 1639 in Alsace; the Jaboulets of the Rhône valley; the Mondavis of California; the Mouton Rothschilds of Bordeaux; Pol Roger, a fourth-generation champagne producer; the Torres family of Spain; and Vega Sicilia of Spain.

Since the original formation, two had to leave the group as they were no longer family-owned: the Mondavis and the Jaboulets. They were replaced by Perrin & Fils, owners of Château de Beaucastel in the Rhône, and Tenuta San Guido, owner of Sassicaia in Tuscany.

## WINE PERSONALITIES

**Veuve Cliquot (1777–1866), the champagne widow**
The widow Cliquot made the champagne house of her name world-famous through several bold business moves. She is famous for having invented a technique for riddling champagne to speed up *dégorgement* (the removal of the sediment of the secondary fermentation, a very slow and wasteful hand process) through the invention of the riddling rack. She is also recognised for her business success in the late eighteenth and early nineteenth centuries, when women did not as a rule participate in commerce.

**Robert Mondavi (1913–2008), the king of Napa**
Robert Mondavi was the son of Italian immigrants and grew up in a wine family. He was a tireless promoter of his wines and the wider brands of Napa and California, and is widely acknowledged as a key part of the success and renown of Napa Valley today. Mondavi was a technical innovator and promoted wine by varietal, now a custom throughout the new world.

## Robert Parker (born 1947), the emperor of wine

Robert Parker was the first wine critic to rate wines on a point scale out of 100 and actively blind taste and rate wines according to his taste rather than based on their historic importance, classification and price. He started his now famous wine review 'The Wine Advocate' part-time while keeping his day job as an advocate. His review of the vintage 1982 of Bordeaux shot him to fame as he recommended buying it while most of the other critics did not. It turned out to be a superb vintage and those who bought on his advice enjoyed fine wine and made great returns. In his heyday Parker was the most powerful wine critic and could move the wine market with a stroke of his pen. He has sold his newsletter to investors based in Singapore and is winding down his active participation in the business. It is questionable whether The Wine Advocate will continue to wield such power without the powerful Parker personality at the helm.

## Jancis Robinson (born 1950), the empress of wine

Jancis Robinson is a wine writer who was the first person outside the wine trade to become a master of wine. She rose to public fame through a 1995 BBC series on wine. She is wine writer for the *Financial Times*, editor of *The Oxford Companion to Wine* (considered the best wine encyclopedia on the market) and also heads up her own online wine website www.jancisrobinson.com.

## Wolf Blass (born 1934), the Irreverent

Wolf Blass Wines was started by Wolfgang Blass, a German immigrant who arrived in Australia with no money and a diploma in wine. To raise awareness of his brand, every time Blass caught a plane or met people at an airport, he requested a call for 'Wolf Blass to come to the arrivals hall' – his way of making people familiar with his name so if they saw his wine on the shelf they would think, 'Oh, haven't I heard this somewhere before? Maybe I'll try it.' He is famous for his garish suits and bow ties, and on winning one of his early awards he shocked the staid crowd by claiming: 'My wines are sexy! They make strong women weak and weak men strong.'

His business went public more than three decades ago but Wolf Blass remains an ambassador for the brand and is an active character in wine circles.

## Celebrities dabbling in wine

Famous celebrities have deep enough pockets to afford the equipment and advice that can help to make fine wine, but a trawl through celebrity wine reviews leaves the impression that if you are after quality you might want to look elsewhere.

| Celebrity | Location of Vineyard |
| --- | --- |
| Brad Pitt and Angelina Jolie | France |
| Antonio Banderas | Spain |
| Drew Barrymore | Italy |
| Gérard Depardieu | France |
| Cliff Richard | Portugal |
| Madonna | USA |
| Sting | Italy |
| David and Victoria Beckham | USA |
| Olivia Newton-John | Australia |
| Sam Neill | New Zealand |

## WINE MOVIES

There are fun wine movies and then there are some documentaries that are perhaps more for wine geeks. This is a small selection of classics.

### A Good Year

A romantic comedy drama starring Russell Crowe and directed by Ridley Scott. The beautiful Provençal vineyard scenery makes watching this film a pleasure but it is also a chick flick complete with a love story. The film was shot at Château La Canorgue, an organic vineyard near Bonnieux, worth a visit for their wines if you are in the area.

### French Kiss

A romantic comedy starring Meg Ryan, Kevin Kline and Jean Reno, with a backdrop of vineyards and a touch of vineyard passion, some unexpected twists and a wine story.

### Sideways

*Sideways* is a hilarious wine lover's cult classic that lambasts Merlot and deifies Pinot Noir. One to watch for a good story and a great laugh. Watch it for the irony too – while lambasting Merlot throughout the film, the iconic bottle the lead character keeps referring to, a Cheval Blanc 1961, is in fact a Merlot blend.

## WHEN IS A PINOT NOIR
## NOT A PINOT NOIR?

After the success of *Sideways*, sales of Merlot-based wines in the USA dropped significantly (some articles suggested they decreased by a third) and Pinot Noir sales rose even more than that, though some of the wine sold as 'Pinot Noir' was not Pinot Noir. Vineyards take several years to grow, and the world's stock of Pinot Noir vineyards could not have changed overnight the way the consumption stats did.

The American wine buyers and consumers drinking the fraudulent wine had no complaints about the product, but the Direction Générale de la Concurrence, de la Consommation et de la Répression des Fraudes, a department of the French government with a dedicated police force (the fraud squad), picked it up: with them, even a loose marketing statement could land you in jail. Selling a blend of Merlot and Shiraz (or Syrah, as Shiraz is called in France) as Pinot Noir resulted in a suspended jail sentence with a fine of over €50,000 for the businessmen in Languedoc-Roussillon who masterminded the fraud.

*Bottle Shock*

*Bottle Shock* tells the true story of an American city professional, Jim Barrett, who went wine-farming in the Napa Valley before it became famous. On the opposite side of the Atlantic, a Paris-based wine-shop owner and now famous English wine journalist, Steven Spurrier (played by Alan Rickman), was concocting a way to improve sales by bringing in high-quality international wines. He decided to raise the prestige of his shop and his new line with a competition between French and Californian wines. On his trip to Napa he meets Barrett, who wants nothing to do with the competition, but his son Bo slips Spurrier a few bottles. In the meantime, the wine concerned does a volte-face and goes brown. Barrett drinks himself into depressed oblivion and gives all the bottles away. In these scenes *Bottle Shock* perfectly captures the angst of being a winemaker. Spurrier, in the meantime, enters the Chardonnay Bo Barrett had given him in the famous Judgement of Paris competition.

When I asked the real Steven Spurrier what he thought of the film, he said: 'More bullshit than *Bottle Shock*.' The base story is true but with a good dose of Hollywood and a little romance injected.

Now the real story from George Taber's (the only journalist present at the tasting) book *The Judgement of Paris* has been bought by a screenwriter named Robert Kamen and is being turned into a film. They will make an interesting side-by-side view on this piece of wine history.

### The Secret of Santa Vittoria

For lovers of old movies, this 1969 film starring Anthony Quinn is about an Italian winegrowing community who succeed in saving a million bottles of their wine from the Nazis in World War Two.

## DOCUMENTARY-STYLE FILMS – THE WINE GEEK SELECTION

### Mondovino

A documentary film by Jonathan Nossiter that explores the globalisation of wine. It offers great contrasts between the big Bordeaux vineyards and the small, family-run Burgundy vineyards, the newly minted billionaires in Napa Valley and the ancient Italian wine dynasties in Florence.

### Natural Resistance

Another documentary from Jonathan Nossiter, this time exploring natural wine in Italy.

*Somm*
A documentary that covers four candidates preparing for the exam that leads to the coveted Master Sommelier Diploma.

*Red Obsession*
An Australian documentary, narrated by Russell Crowe, that charts red wine across the globe from Bordeaux to China and everywhere in between.

## BOOKS FOR ENTERTAINMENT AND LEARNING ABOUT WINE

*The Battle for Wine and Love* by Alice Feiring
A mix of anecdotes and interesting people in the wine world, with a dose of why natural wine is good, by *The New York Times* wine writer.

*Red, White, and Drunk All Over* by Natalie MacLean
A voyage of both old and new stories about wine; some very amusing.

*The Billionaire's Vinegar* by Benjamin Wallace
An investigative journalist delves into the world of auctions for fine wines. A page-turning exposé that has been made into a film.

*Wine and War* by Don and Petie Kladstrup
The French, the Nazis and the battle for one of France's greatest treasures – wine – during World War Two. A gripping and informative history.

*The Widow Cliquot* by Tilar J. Mazzeo
A wonderful history of how the Veuve Cliquot champagne empire was created and the woman who ruled it, inverting the social norms of the day.

*The Emperor of Wine: The Rise of Robert M. Parker Jr*
**by Elin McCoy**
This is a fascinating picture of how Robert Parker rose to become the most powerful wine critic in the world and his impact on the wine world.

*The House of Mondavi* **by Julia Flynn Siler**
This book includes family feuds that make *Dallas* look tame but makes for intriguing reading into how Robert Mondavi built his winery and how he eventually lost it.

*Wine Wars* **by Mike Veseth**
An exploration of wine and the cultural and economic forces in the wine world. An easy and very informative read.

## A YEAR IN PROVENCE-STYLE BOOKS ABOUT VINEYARDS

*Grape Expectations* **by Caro Feely**
A story of a family's life change from city professionals to farmers – part personal story, part technical information about how grapes are grown and wine is made, and a business story of the struggle to create a new business.

*Saving our Skins* **by Caro Feely**
The story of the turnaround from a struggling vineyard to a sustainable, thriving business, plus their progress

with organic farming and initiation into biodynamic viticulture.

*A Vineyard in Tuscany* by **Ferenc Máté**
Written with humour and intrigue, this book tells the story of Ferenc and his wife Candace moving from New York City to restore a friary and vineyard in Tuscany.

*The Ripening Sun* by **Patricia Atkinson**
Patricia Atkinson and her husband left London city jobs to restore a house and four hectares of vines in the Dordogne in the 1990s. This is the story of Patricia's success against great challenges, including the departure of her husband early on in the adventure. She built the tiny property into a thriving 21-hectare vineyard.

## CONCLUSION

Learning about wine in a leisurely way through books and films is a great way to gain wine wisdom. Perhaps these films and books will start you on a journey that inspires you to go further – even to move on to wine text books. There are other ways to fine tune your skills including wine school and wine tasting holidays.

# CHAPTER 9

# FINDING OUT MORE

· · · · · · · · · · · · · · · · · · · · · · · · · · · · · · · · · · · · · · · · · · · · · · · · ·

Wine knowledge is like taking a sip of wine, it begs for more. If you want to go deeper to take your wine senses to the next level there are many great ways to do it starting with being more adventurous in your wine choices and going on to wine holidays and to wine school.

# GOING WINE TASTING ON YOUR HOLIDAYS: A GREAT WAY TO LEARN ABOUT WINE

A holiday on a wine route is magnificent, historic and fun – and if you take your car and stock up on wine the trip will be partially funded by the savings you make. Nowhere can you experience wines better than on the *terroir* itself. Exploring a French wine region in particular is a heavenly holiday. It offers the double benefit of pleasure and stocking your cellar with wine at French prices. Here are a few guidelines to get you started…

At one time wine-touring in France was daunting if your French was scratchy or non-existent. Now enough winemakers speak English that this is no longer an issue. Wine-route maps typically indicate what languages the winemaker speaks (you can get these from the local tourist office or *maison des vins* in all the wine regions – if you are really organised you can even email them for a copy in advance).

The more you explore, the more rewards (apart from the wine) you will find, from a hidden cellar in a cave that has housed wines since pre-medieval times to a real druid's chair to a *grand cru classé* farmed with horses to a cellar with a pencil drawing from the French Revolution alongside a seventh-century grain silo.

If you are going in tourist season (May–September) make sure you book your accommodation in advance. August and September can be difficult for appointments if there are specific estates you want to see, as August is typically when winemakers take a brief summer holiday and September is the harvest. However you will still find winemakers willing to open their doors to you if you are flexible about exactly when you visit. October can be a good month as the summer tourism crowds have abated and your wine treasures won't cook on the journey home.

While some estates in France are large enough to have full-time staff in the tasting room, these are sometimes less interesting as you don't get to meet the winemaker. The downside of the smaller estates is that you need to plan ahead. An email or phone call to fix a time (even if just the day before) can be all it takes to be sure that you will be welcomed and that your *vigneron* won't be out on their tractor in yonder parcel.

Most wine estates in France don't charge for wine tasting as it is seen as a marketing activity. This does mean there is some pressure to at least buy some wine. In a wide tasting across an estate's wines there is sure to be something that you like enough to buy, even if it is just a couple of bottles. Wines from a place you have visited have an added dimension of enjoyment and offer a good story for a dinner party.

A tour of the vineyard and winery can be entertaining for kids as long as you don't dally on the tasting bit, expecting them to hang around for hours while you discuss the finer nuances of each vintage with the winemaker. Some wine estates include a playground. At Château de Monbazillac, a medieval castle near Bergerac, you can tour the castle and surrounds then have a wine tasting while the kids enjoy some grape juice.

Arm yourself with two good books on the region – a tourism guide and a winegrower guide. We found that wine-routing provided such an authentic and historic experience in France that it catered for both wine and tourism. Before becoming winegrowers ourselves we would scour our winegrower guides and notes gathered from newspaper and magazine articles for good places to visit before leaving home then do more sleuthing for gems once we were installed in France. If you are serious about visiting several properties in a day, spitting at the wine tastings is obligatory even if it goes against the grain (French police have tightened up enforcement of drink-driving rules).

That brings us to a key question: which region? I would recommend starting in a region where there are excellent wines but also great tourism opportunities, so you get a balanced holiday. My pick for regions that offer both of these in France are the Loire Valley and the Dordogne Valley (the latter being a part of the greater region referred to as South West France by most wine books).

## LUXURY OR BUDGET

Wine, particularly in France, is seen as part of the *art de vivre* and culture – fortunately, both can be enjoyed at almost any budget. A wonderful holiday can be had camping and visiting small rising stars that are creating masterful wine symphonies on a tight budget, or staying in five-star luxury and visiting *grands crus*.

For a casual, budget holiday with a little more comfort than camping, try staying for a week or two in a gîte (self-catering holiday house) in the heart of wine country and touring from there. With self-catering you can also make the most of the excellent fresh food available from French markets (matched impeccably, of course, with your daily wine purchases). Some estates offer packed picnics or allow customers to picnic on-site.

If you have already toured wine country in California, South Africa or Australia you may find wine touring in France quite undeveloped and authentic. France boasts multitudes of small producers who offer a delightfully close look into the window of French wine, culture, life and that elusive concept of *terroir*. Bon voyage!

## WINE SCHOOL

To gain a more structured knowledge fine-tune your skills; a wine course with your local wine shop or through an organisation like the Wine Spirit Education Trust with one of their approved programme providers (WSET APP) can help significantly. Wine is an enormous subject that is difficult to categorise but WSET achieves this very well. The first level offers a gentle introduction to formal wine tasting focused on varietals. Level two takes you into wines of the world. Level three explores more regions; more complex tastings and includes a blind tasting exam along with the theory exam. These formal programmes are a good step to going forward with more confidence. Attending your local wine shop's tasting sessions and winemaker nights offers a less formal way to garner some of this knowledge. Beyond these lighter programmes are the more serious Diploma of Wine, Master of Wine and Sommelier qualifications.

# YOUR OWN WINE RESEARCH

There are many great resources on the internet that offer hours of free education. Here are a few that I use regularly:

- www.jancisrobinson.com
- www.wineanorak.com
- www.thewinedoctor.com
- www.winefolly.com

For regional wine guides about growers in a particular area an internet search will yield the best and latest information but a printed guide can be very useful.

## CONCLUSION

Wine holidays and wine school are like a breath of fresh air into your wine world. Even for wine professionals they offer a fresh view on your world of wine and a reminder of why we love wine.

# CONCLUSION

This book may be a taster, or the start or continuation of your exploration of wine – an immense and complex world. Even the most expert of experts Jancis Robinson says she learns something new about wine every day.

Not only is it an already large and complex world, but it is constantly evolving. It is changing to take into account wine lovers' demands, economic and environmental challenges like global warming, and better use of new technologies. A recent study showed that 40 years from now, Montpellier, in the south of France, is likely to be growing grapes that do well in Palermo, Sicily, now; perhaps in 40 years then, Bordeaux and Bergerac will be growing the grapes they grow in Montpellier today.

One thing is certain: as a wine lover, with the diversity of wine already available and this constant evolution, you will not be bored. I challenge you to step out of your fixed favourites and meet each new wine as a potential friend. Wines are as different as people: there will be some you don't appreciate as much as others and some you love, but the exploration will be a delight in itself. Give each wine the moment of reflection they deserve, given their heritage and the work that went into them. Here's to more wine adventures and to great moments shared around a bottle of wine! May your wine journey be filled with joy.

# ABOUT THE
# AUTHOR

......................................................

Caro Feely can usually be found juggling vineyard, wine school, writing and ecological accommodation in South West France. She is an author, wine teacher, speaker on agriculture and wine, and biodynamic winegrower. She and husband Sean grow organic and natural wines and most of their own food with the help of their daughters Sophia and Ellie. You can find out more about the vineyard at www.FeelyWines.com, about the accommodation at www.LuxuryDordogneGites.com and about the wine school and tours at www.FrenchWineAdventures.com. No matter what she is juggling at the end of the day, one hand usually has a glass of wine in it.

# GRAPE EXPECTATIONS

*'a beautifully written tale of passion and guts'*
Alice Feiring, author of *Naked Wine*

A Family's
Vineyard Adventure
in France

Château Haut Garrigue

Caro Feely

# GRAPE EXPECTATIONS

A Family's Vineyard Adventure in France

Caro Feely

ISBN: 978 1 84953 257 0
Paperback
£9.99

When Caro and Sean find the perfect ten-hectare vineyard in Saussignac, it seems their dreams of becoming winemakers in the south of France are about to come true. But, rather than making a smooth transition from city slickers to *connaisseurs du vin*, they arrive in France with their young family (a toddler and a newborn) to be faced with a dilapidated eighteenth-century farmhouse and 'beyond eccentric' winery. Undeterred by a series of setbacks, including mouse infestations and a nasty accident with an agricultural trimmer, they embark on the biggest adventure of their lives – learning to make wine from the roots up.

*'A must-read for anyone who's dreamed of owning their own vineyard… an inspiring story of how one couple changed their lives.'*

Jamie Ivey, author of *Extremely Pale Rosé*

# Saving Our Skins

## Building a Vineyard Dream in France

### CARO FEELY

# SAVING OUR SKINS

## Building a Vineyard Dream in France

Caro Feely

ISBN: 978 1 84953 609 7
Paperback
£8.99

Frost can be fatal to a fledgling wine business... gorgeous glitter with a high price tag. On a winter's day it is beautiful, but on a spring day after bud burst it means devastation. For Seán and Caro Feely, a couple whose love affair with wine and France has taken them through financial and physical struggle to create their organic vineyard, it could spell the end. Until they receive an unexpected call that could save their skins...

This tale is about life, love and taking risks, while transforming a piece of land into a flourishing vineyard and making a new life in France.

*'could inspire you to... move to the backwaters of France, and bet your life, all for the love of making wine'*

Alice Feiring, author of *Naked Wine*

Have you enjoyed this book?
If so, why not write a review on your favourite website?

If you're interested in finding out more about our books,
find us on Facebook at **Summersdale Publishers** and
follow us on Twitter at **@Summersdale**.

Thanks very much for buying this Summersdale book.

**www.summersdale.com**